The Drake Beam Morin Guide to Retirement Planning

DBM PUBLISHING

A DIVISION OF DRAKE BEAM MORIN, INC.

100 Park Avenue
New York NY 10017
212 692-7700
800 345-5627

Printed in the United States of America
ISBN 1-880030-28-4

Table of Contents

1. Retirement: Not What It Used to Be 5

2. Your Finances—The Key Issues 16

3. Your Health: Wealth is Useless Without It 36

4. What Will You Do With All That Time? 48

5. To Work or Not to Work? 57

6. The Leisure Smorgasbord 79

7. Changing Roles/Relationships 91

8. To Move or Not to Move: Still Another Question 105

9. Lifetime Action Planning 126

About Drake Beam Morin, Inc. 141

Retirement: Not What It Used to Be

1

Like the old gray mare, retirement "ain't what it used to be." But unlike the old gray mare, it's gotten more spirited and active, not less so.

Think about the typical retirement of a generation or two ago (such as your parents' or grandparents'). Retirement then was seen as the end of an active, useful life: the slow withdrawal from vital, exciting activities and meaningful work. People who retired sat around, if not in a rocker, then a recliner, watched TV, played a little golf, had a few lunches out for excitement or caught the senior citizens' bargain matinee at the movies. The typical retiree was 65, which meant that a couple of generations ago, when life expectancies were lower, the typical retirement only lasted five or ten years before the retiree passed on.

Today's retirement is a new beginning. It's a time to be free of the restraints imposed by others and actively pursue your own goals. People are retiring younger, in response to these personal goals or often because of company-offered early retirement programs. Many of these people are healthier and more energetic than earlier generations, and ambitious enough to work full- or part-time for other companies or start their own consulting practices or small businesses.

When you factor in these earlier retirements to today's longer life expectancies, you find that many people will be "retired" for almost as long as they worked, perhaps 20-30 years. It's been referred to as "the third half of life" because there are so many options. Some of these options for today's active retiree:

- Start a small business
- Return to school for a degree or to pursue an area of strong personal interest
- Work part-time (or even full-time for a new company or in a second career)
- Begin an ambitious physical fitness program (for example, there is an increasing number of marathon runners in their 50's, 60's and 70's, a phenomenon that would make your grandma or grandpa shake their head in disbelief if they could be around to see it)
- Actively manage an investment portfolio
- Travel the region, the country or the world to research the family tree and write a book of family memoirs
- Perhaps even engage in the "traditional" retirement activities of leisure, volunteering, increased family involvement

These increased options mean that the old model of life planning no longer applies. In that model, life was divided into three discrete stages, in each of which a particular activity dominated to the virtual exclusion of all others. For the first 20-25 years that activity was learning. For the middle years that activity was work. And for the later retirement years the focus was on leisure. Figure 1 presents a "picture" of this life planning model.

In the new life planning model (Figure 2), these phases blend into each other. The "boxes" merge. College students combine work with their studies or take a few years off from school to experience the "real world." The middle-aged attend school or receive specialized training while they pursue their careers; and leisure is not put off until retirement (there are lots of 40-year-olds in the marathon, too!).

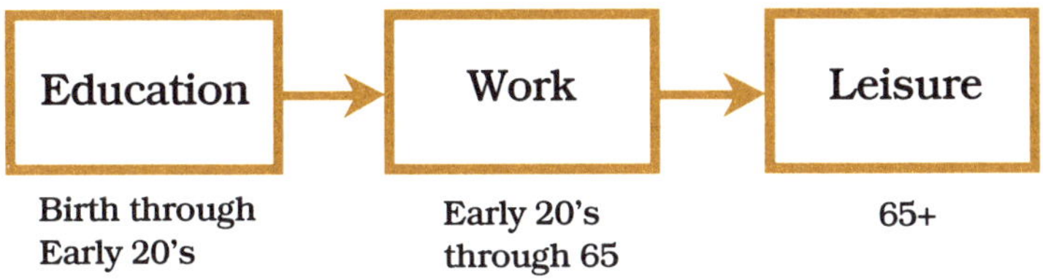

- A linear progression
- One phase was completed before next began

Figure 1 Former Life Planning Model

And retirement, while maintaining a large leisure component, is not limited to bridge, shuffleboard and golf. Few retirees pursue or want a life of total leisure; it lacks excitement and stimulation. Most pursue a mix of leisure, learning and work activities (paid or volunteer, part-time or full-time, working for others or running their own business).

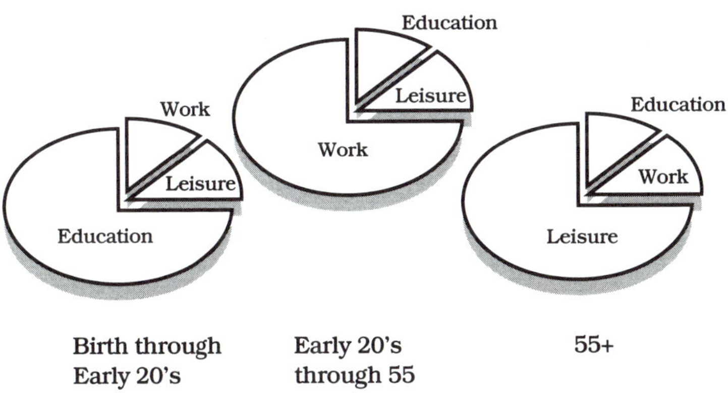

- Less linear
- Several activities at each stage

Figure 2 New Life Planning Model

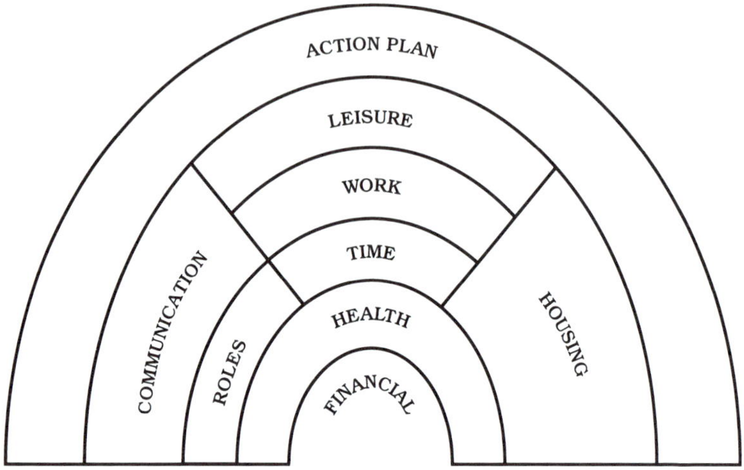

Figure 3 The Retirement Arch

Building Your Retirement: The Retirement Arch

Because retirements are so different today and because there's no single blueprint that will work for everyone, you've got to build your own customized retirement plan in the same way you built and implemented a career plan. Drake Beam Morin, Inc. has devised the Retirement Arch to reflect these new realities and help you arrive at your own plan. If you address each piece of the arch, you will find that the "third half" of your life meets your ideal mix of needs for challenge, excitement, satisfaction and perhaps even a little rest.

If you fail to address or plan for one segment of the arch, you'll find that the whole structure becomes a little wobbly. That's because, as in a real stone arch, the different segments support and interrelate with each other. If your finances are not in order, you may not have the money you need to keep yourself healthy or pursue travel or leisure goals. If you have picked the wrong housing options (such as trying to maintain an older, large home you no longer need), you could find all your time and money being spent on home repair.

Let's look at the segments of the arch and how they connect with each other.

Financial Planning. This is a basic building block of retirement. It's difficult to achieve many retirement goals without adequate financial planning. Financial planning affects whether and how much you will work, how easily you will meet your health needs, how you'll spend your leisure time and the type of housing you'll have at various stages in your retirement.

Health. There's an Arab proverb that states, "Whoever has health has everything." If you're in poor or severely declining health, your leisure options are curtailed (no trip to Europe or weekly game of tennis). Health also affects the ability to work, and retirees in declining health often are forced out of independent living situations and into more supervised settings.

If you have abused your body through long working hours, bad eating habits, overuse of alcohol, caffeine and drugs, it is still not too late to begin a healthy regimen which restores your vitality in your later years. It's not always easy to change the habits of a lifetime, but to paraphrase Art Linkletter, "the new retirement is not for sissies." If you are committed to the goal of better health, retirement can be one of the most opportune times to achieve it, since you are more in control of your own schedule and habits.

Time. Time is a resource, just like money and health. However, many retirees waste this precious resource because they fail to establish priorities and a schedule which assures that they meet these priorities. The worst thing for many of us to face is a huge block of empty space in our calendars which work used to occupy. The chapter on time management will help you manage your retirement time so that this space is not just "filled up," but rather is structured and planned so that time is spent in the activities and goals *you* wish to pursue.

Work. Maynard G. Krebs, the beatnik character on the situation comedy "Dobie Gillis," used to have an aversive reaction to this word. Perhaps as a retiree you are also questioning why this word should be associated in any way with retirement. But working in retirement is becoming increasingly common. This is because:

- For many retirees, a pension needs to be supplemented by extra income
- Many retirees feel less than effective, even "useless," when they are not working for pay
- Many retirees feel work adds needed structure to their lives
- Some retirees miss the social aspects of working and feel more connected to the world when they are in the workplace either full- or part-time
- For many, retirement is the opportunity to pursue a second career or a business which represents a lifelong interest or passion

If you choose to work during retirement, you will find many other people at your age and stage pursuing work-related activities, usually on their own terms and determining their own schedules and levels of commitment.

Leisure. Yes, there's still time for recreation and fun in retirement. But for today's healthier, more active retirees, there are more options, which can make the choices more confusing. The "health" and "financial" segments of the arch have a lot to do with the choices you make in this area.

Roles and Relationships. The change in one's roles and relationships is often the most overlooked challenge for many retirees. You will be losing the role of full-time company employee, and with it much of your identity and many of your social contacts. What will you replace this with?

The hours you formerly spent in work-related activities (10 hours a day or more) will now be spent with friends, family and alone. How well-prepared are you for this? How many friends do you really have outside of work? How much time do you really want to spend with your partner and the rest of your family? ("I married him for better or worse, but not for lunch!") These decisions should be consciously made and executed, not just "fallen into," so that you are in control of your own retirement.

Communication. To achieve your retirement goals, you'll have to communicate with a different mix of people than when you were working: friends, family, lawyer, doctor, financial planner, other retirees. By honing your communication and networking skills, you ensure that you convey your wishes and needs to this new cast of characters and get the information you need from them.

Communication can help you define your retirement roles and relationships so you know what to expect from others and they know what to expect from you: no surprises!

Housing. Whether you remain in your present location or residence interrelates with a number of factors. Is it financially to your advantage to sell and move to a less expensive home or area? Do you need to live near family or a major population center? What type of health and community services do you need? This chapter will help you make informed decisions in this area, both in your earlier retirement years and for later, when your needs may change.

Action Planning. When you have completed this book, you will write an action plan which covers every aspect of your retirement. What are your goals and what are the steps you plan to take to achieve them? The written action plan can serve as a blueprint as you begin your retirement, and it can be adjusted periodically as your needs and goals change.

Making the Transition to Retirement

Life is full of transitions: from home to elementary school, from high school to college, from college to career and from full-time career to retirement. Some transitions are easier than others, but all have in common a series of predictable stages. These stages are Reconcilement, Reorientation and Recommitment.

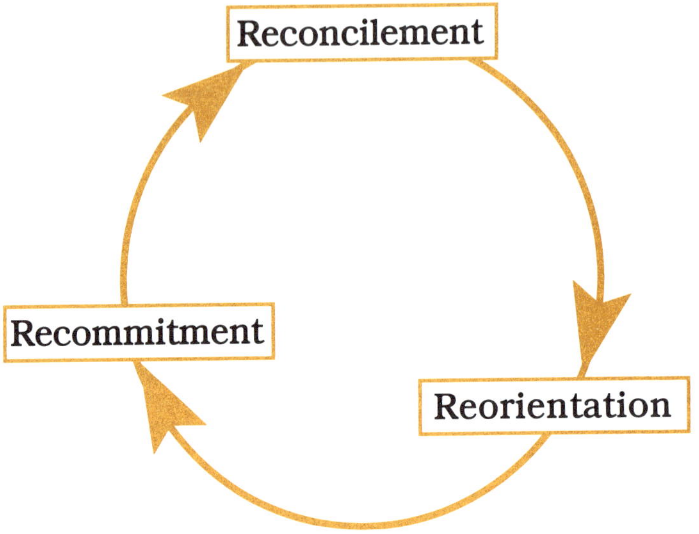

Figure 4 Transition Model

Reconcilement

When a period of life or a cherished relationship comes to an end, most people have a difficult time "letting go" of it. During this time of learning to become reconciled, called the "ending" by some theorists, one can feel sadness mixed with anger over the loss. As a retiree, you may be giving up:

- Your identity as a corporate employee
- A place to go every day where people know and respect you
- Daily acknowledgment of your work accomplishments
- A set of well-defined responsibilities

It is sometimes difficult to let the past go and move on. For many people, reconcilement may be achieved within a few weeks; for others, it takes more time. Ending a long career can diminish a person's self-image: no longer can the retiree say , "I'm a __________ and I work for ________." The key to successfully negotiating the reconcilement stage is to understand that the desire to hang on to the "old" identity is normal and predictable, while acknowledging and acting on the need to move ahead to the next stage. Those who may have the hardest time with the career-ending transition are those who have been most heavily committed to work; people who have applied their energies wholeheartedly at their jobs may have to struggle to let go of their old identity—the full-time corporate employee—before they can adapt to their new identity—retiree.

On the other hand, those who have considered retirement for years have been preparing themselves for the reconcilement phase. Individuals who have already begun to transfer their interest and non-working time to hobbies, sports, socializing and other activities will make an easier transition. Most people are somewhere in between the extremes of clinging to a work-oriented identity and easily letting go of it; they have balanced their work commitments and leisure activities. For these people, ending careers will involve some readjustment and a moderate amount of time.

Reorientation

During this phase (known by some theorists as the "Neutral Zone") the retiree has accepted the reality of change and the loss of the old identity and activities, but has yet to develop something to take their place. It is characterized by a feeling of being "in limbo," restlessness, questioning of life's purpose and the effort to restructure time around meaningful goals. This phase, while often uncomfortable, is almost always temporary.

At this point, the retiree needs the support of others, as well as time alone to assess the new situation; he or she may feel sadness or confusion. The orientation phase is not a time of high energy or creativity; while the retiree is still forming a new identity, it is not wise to act precipitously.

Retirees should recognize this phase when they experience it and use this time to consider what they really want to do in the next 20 to 30 years. They should carefully evaluate the direction and actions that they will take in the next phase—Recommitment.

Recommitment

This phase is reached when you embrace your new role (in this case, retiree) and feel ready to make a "new beginning." You are able to visualize the next chapter in your life. This stage is characterized by an increasingly clear direction and the energy and confidence to carry out a new Life Plan; new goals are defined, as well as the strategies for achieving them. Backward glances will be taken less frequently as new activities and relationships emerge. An understanding of the transition process and the time it takes may help you in your move from full-time employee to retiree and make a better overall adjustment to retirement and any other major changes in your life.

Exercise 1. Personal Reflections

Complete the following statements to help you pinpoint the retirement issues that most concern you and need the most attention and planning.

1. Retirement to me means
2. My main concern now is
3. Financially, I am
4. My goal for the future is
5. Looking back, I'm happiest about
6. My biggest regret is
7. A productive life means
8. I wish my family (spouse)
9. One change I plan to make in retirement is
10. My objectives for retirement are:

    a.

    b.

    c.

    d.

Exercise 2. Visualize Your Retirement

Create a mental picture of yourself as a retiree in the next few years. In what activities are you engaged? What percentage of your time do you devote to each one? How do you look and feel? Who are your companions? (Describe the first pictures that come to mind.)

Activity	Percentage of Time	With Whom

Consider how your parents (or anyone important in your life) retired. Did they enjoy it? Did they move? How did it compare to the work phase of their lives? What challenges did they face? Is their retirement a positive or negative example?

Mother

Father

Key relatives or others

Your Finances— The Key Issues

2

Questions To Ask Yourself

By asking yourself the following questions, you will gauge how thoroughly you have planned your retirement finances and identify areas that need attention.

1. Do I have a general financial plan for my retirement based on a realistic projection of my retirement income and expenses?

2. Do I have a competent, unbiased financial advisor or know where to get one quickly?

3. Have I allowed for inflation in planning my retirement finances?

4. Do I know my approximate net worth: the value of all my assets reduced by the value of all my liabilities?

5. Do I understand the various payment options of my company's pension plan and the amounts I will receive if electing particular options?

6. Do I know how much Social Security I will receive when I become eligible?

7. Have I reviewed my investments in light of my decision to retire, and am I considering appropriate changes?

8. Do I know if I will need to do some paid work to meet my financial goals, and how much I would have to earn?

9. Am I well informed about any changes in my company medical benefits due to retirement and the possible need for supplementary coverage?

10. Have I prepared the proper documents to assure that my property will be transferred to the people I choose, and do I know the location of vital supporting documents, such as wills, birth and marriage certificates?

Will You Have Enough Money in Retirement?

In the ideal fantasy world, all our decisions would be made without regard to money. We'd just do exactly what we wanted to do: all day, all night, all year, all our lives.

But let's face it, most of us don't live in an ideal world. A major part of the reason we worked was for the money and what it represented: physical survival, achievement of important personal goals, helping our families grow and develop long-term financial security.

While you were working, you had a steady paycheck and benefits such as health insurance. You adapted your spending habits to that compensation package. Retirement represents a dramatic change in your financial picture, and you may be wondering how your lifestyle may have to change to match your changed income and benefits.

It's such a daunting change that many retirees respond by sticking their heads in the sand. "Planning is too complicated; there are too many variables. Let's just wing it, take it a month at a time." When you fail to plan and analyze your finances, you can fall into two traps. The first is to continue your present lifestyle (or even expand on it) even though your income has been reduced. "We waited this long for retirement. Let's take a few cruises and buy that luxury car we always wanted. You only live once, you can't take it with you, and we may not live much longer anyway." The catch in living like there's no tomorrow is that you may have *many* tomorrows, and without analyzing your income and outgo you may outlive your resources. To put it another way, you may run out of money.

The second financial trap is to go into an uninformed panic. "Our biggest source of steady income is gone, and we'll never make another penny again. Our only resource is my pension, and it may have to last us 30 years. Travel and vacations are out of the question. Let's start buying our clothes at second-hand shops. Come to think of it, who really needs clothes?"

An objective analysis of your retirement finances can avoid either of these extremes. By looking at your projected income and outgo, you can formulate a rational budget and spending plan during this "third half of life" which ensures that you achieve your goals in all areas without impoverishing yourself or living in self-imposed austerity.

This chapter covers the basic issues you need to address in creating a financial plan for your retirement years. It is not a substitute for serious research and reading on the more technical areas of financial planning or consultation with a financial planner. It does not give specific financial advice. It simply points out all the areas and questions you will want to address in order to make informed financial decisions during retirement.

Basic Financial Issues

Financial planning in retirement is structured around two goals:

- Minimization of taxes in a legal manner
- Commitment of assets to investments that provide minimal risk to insure that projected expenses can be met

Key concerns include:

- Allowing for inflation
- Estimating your retirement expenses and assuring that sufficient money will be available when it is needed

To plan for your retirement, you will analyze your net worth (assets and liabilities), your anticipated income and your expenses to arrive at a plan that works for you.

Choosing a Financial Advisor

Financial planning is best done in personal consultation with a competent financial advisor. This book's review of basic issues is not a substitute for such consultation; it is a summary of key issues you will want to think about and discuss with an advisor.

Here are general descriptions of several types of advisors.

- **Personal Financial Planners.** A recent development is the Certified Planner (certified via exams given by the College of Financial Planning in Denver). These advisors have a couple of associations to help legitimize their profession, and they advertise their services. Your local Yellow Pages probably lists dozens of "Financial Planning Consultants." Remember that credentials alone do not guarantee that a planner has the experience and skill to meet your particular needs.

- **Investment Advisors.** They cover the full range of assets. Some will offer to take your nest egg and manage it through a portfolio of assorted investments — stocks, bonds, tax exemptions, Certificates of Deposit, Treasury Bills, annuities, tax shelters, etc. Others will advocate precious metals, income properties, stamps, or fine art.

  Aside from the question of their expertise, some investment advisors also sell products. They may be faced with a conflict between what you need and what they sell. It is difficult to find an absolutely objective investment advisor.

- **Tax Accountants and Tax Attorneys.** The tax accountant can help you predict the tax effect of your investments and other financial maneuvers. Since tax laws and rulings are frequently changed, you need to be sure you are taking advantage of the tax-avoidance opportunities under the law. If your financial affairs are complex, you probably already have an accountant preparing your tax returns. This person can be an important part of your financial planning team, and you should encourage him or her to participate creatively. These advisors are often part of a firm of Certified Public Accountants.

Tax attorneys often cover the same ground, including preparation of tax returns and offering tax-saving advice. They have added expertise in interpreting the tax laws and court rulings as applied to your special problems and their services may cost you more. They usually work in law firms. You will especially need an attorney familiar with taxes if you are setting up your own business during retirement.

- **Insurance Advisors.** Life insurance can be protection and an investment. If you have older policies with an investment component, you may be earning a very low interest rate and it could pay you to convert or liquidate such policies. When leaving a company, you often have a brief period in which to convert group insurance to an individual policy. Look into your insurance situation at your earliest opportunity.

  In addition to ensuring your, and your spouse's income needs, you should also look into your overall protection against liability, accident, medical costs, fire, theft, etc. It is possible to be overinsured as well as underinsured and you may want to revise your coverage.

  Your insurance planning should be integrated with other phases of your financial planning.

- **Attorneys** (for wills and estates). By bringing up the subject of estate planning, we are not suggesting that since you are now retired, you should start thinking about your imminent death. If you are like most retirees, you will probably live several more decades. However, if you are like most retirees, you have been too busy working to update your will. Because retirement dramatically changes your financial picture and because you now have the time to do so, this is the perfect opportunity to review your will and estate plan. Estate planning is simply your provision for distribution of your estate when you die.

A family attorney can handle most wills, even with a form of trust. If your affairs are complex, you may want a tax expert as a part of your advisory team on estate planning.

To choose among these advisors, consider:

- Professional training credentials and experience, particularly in serving people of your age or income
- Their ability to objectively promote the client's interest (e.g., stockbrokers tend to advise buying and selling stock; they may neglect other instruments)
- Honesty and personality—do you instinctively trust and like your advisor?
- Fees—up-front and long-term (fees may be tax deductible)
- How does the advisor keep up-to-date on latest developments in his or her field (subscriptions to magazines and data bases, association membership)?
- Flexibility—is the advisor willing to work with your accountant, lawyer or other professional advisor?
- Availability—how often will you meet with the planner? (If he or she is with a large firm, will you sometimes have to meet with someone else?)
- References—a reputable, competent planner should be happy to supply the names of several references (who may provide answers to the above questions)

Other retirees and executives, your banker, other advisors, professional associations and directories are good sources of candidates' names; also try the Yellow Pages.

Interview the candidates just as if you were hiring them (which you are). See if you can communicate comfortably. Explain your needs and get their reactions.

Don't jump to a decision to hire; shop around a bit. Be aware that small firms are often easier to deal with than large ones. However, large firms may have more resources at their disposal.

Calculating Your Net Worth

In planning for retirement it's important to arrive at an approximation of your net worth; getting expert help usually results in a very accurate assessment. This is done by subtracting what you owe (debts) from what you own (assets). To arrive at this figure, you inventory some, or all, of the following items (different planners may include different items).

Assets

- Cash on hand
- Bank accounts (checking and savings)
- Market value of home
- Other real estate
- Household furnishings
- Current market value of auto
- Savings bonds
- Cash value of life insurance
- Stocks and bonds
- Money in IRA
- Money owed you
- Personal property
- Other

Liabilities

- Balance due on mortgage
- Other loans
- Balance due on credit cards and charge accounts
- Installment debt (e.g., car loan)
- Insurance premiums due
- Taxes owed
- Other current bills and debts

Keep in mind that the total net worth is not instantly available. Your home may be worth $150,000, but if you're not ready to sell it, that money is not currently available to you. Investments that are tied up for a specified length of time are unavailable as well.

A *fixed* asset is one that takes time and effort to sell (i.e., it is not readily convertible into cash); a *liquid* asset can be sold or converted into cash on short notice without sacrificing value (e.g., bank accounts, stocks, precious metals). It is advisable to have the proper combination of liquid and fixed assets so that cash is readily available in an emergency, for predictable expenses, or for a business opportunity.

Why should you calculate your net worth?

- To make you aware of how rich or poor you actually are
- To give your financial advisors the raw data they need
- To remind you of all your investments, bank accounts, etc.—especially useful for your survivors
- To prompt you to update your will
- To point out resources to draw on when/if your income drops below your expenses
- To inform you of what you have tied up in non-earning assets—e.g., a house
- To stimulate consideration of how assets might be redeveloped for better returns

Future Income vs. Expenses

Compare the income you expect against what you need to live on: the difference between the two will be your deficit or surplus.

- A *deficit* occurs when your expenses exceed your income. You can close the gap by increasing earnings or income, by eating into your net worth (including selling assets) or by cutting your expenses.

- A *surplus* is the opposite of deficit. You can use your surplus to build up your capital, nest egg, retirement reserve and/or your estate.

This calculation is, by definition, an approximate projection. It cannot be calculated exactly due to unpredictable expenses, inflation and other uncontrollable factors. However, by arriving at an approximate bottom line, you can estimate if your needs will be met or if you will be "caught short."

The bottom line can help you answer these questions:

- "Do I need to continue working? For how long?"
- "Should I work part- or full-time?"
- "Should my spouse work, too?"
- "Should we reduce expenses? In what areas?"
- "Are there assets we no longer need which could be sold to increase our cash resources during retirement?"
- "Is there enough surplus for discretionary items, such as travel?"

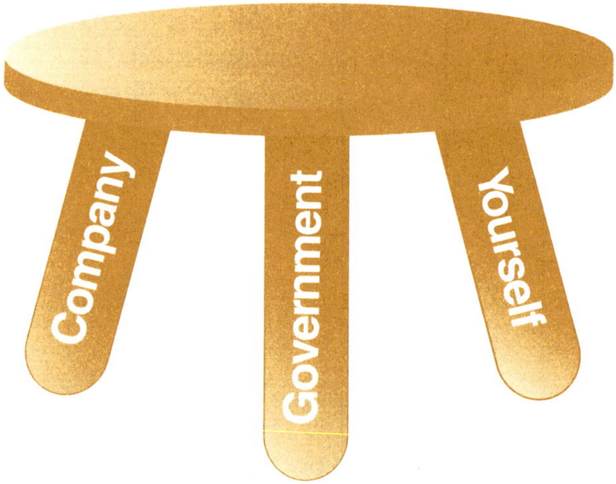

Figure 5 Main Sources of Income for Most Retirees

Income

Your retirement income will probably come from several sources. The three main sources of income for most retirees (often referred to as the "Three-Legged Stool") are your company (pensions and other benefits), the government (Social Security), and yourself (IRAs, savings and investment plans, and any income you or your spouse receive from working).

Your Company: Employer Pension and Profit-sharing Plans

Before you retire, you need to understand your pension plan thoroughly and estimate your benefit. It is a good idea to meet with your company's pension plan administrator to clear up any questions you might have. For example:

- "What is the company's vesting formula?"
- "What will my pension be if I retire now?" (at 65? at 70?)
- "What are my payout options?" (annuity, lump sum)
- "Under what circumstances can the employer change or terminate the plan? Are my benefits guaranteed for life?"
- "What benefits do my survivors receive if I die?"
- "Is the pension plan insured?" (By whom?)
- "If I receive Social Security, will my pension benefits be reduced?"

Here are some important facts about pensions.

- There are two types of pensions: defined benefit and defined contribution. Under a defined benefit plan, participants know the exact amount they will receive. Under a defined contribution plan, the amount paid into the plan is known, but the benefit payout varies, depending on the plan's investment performance and other factors.

- Unlike Social Security, most pension benefits remain the same each year. There is usually no cost of living adjustment (COLA) for inflation.

- A "participant" is not the same as a "recipient." You need to participate in the plan for a certain period before you become vested. A vested employee is entitled to a benefit that cannot be revoked.

- It is easier to become vested than it used to be. Prior to 1976, employers could require employees to work a lifetime before they were vested. Most employers must now provide vesting much sooner. Consult your plan administrator for your company's vesting formula.

- If you elect retirement at an earlier age than is standard with your company, your monthly benefit will be less. (This is because the company will have to pay you for more years.)

- If you divorce, your pension may be considered property of the marriage, and your ex-spouse may be awarded part of it.

- The decision to receive your pension in a lump sum or in monthly checks is a difficult one with many tax implications. You may have the option of an annuity, giving you monthly payments for as long as you live. All options should be discussed thoroughly with an advisor and your pension plan administrator.

- By law, most company pensions must provide a surviving spouse option. Unless you notify the company in writing, the company must provide 100 percent coverage. This degree of coverage results in smaller payments while you and your spouse are both alive; with 50 percent coverage, payments are higher while you are both alive, but lower after you die. Investigate this choice carefully.

- A pension plan may terminate if a company is in serious trouble or cannot afford to continue the plan. If the plan is terminated for some other reason, part or all of your pension benefits may be protected by the Pension Benefit Guarantee Corporation; talk to your plan administrator for more details.

- Some plans contain Social Security integration, under which the base calculation of any pension will be reduced by a part of the Social Security calculation. Find out if this is part of your plan.

- You could lose pension benefits under certain conditions, including return to certain kinds of work, divorce, plan termination or changes, or receipt of other retirement benefits. Check with your plan administrator for details.

You may want to look at the documents listed below to learn more about your pension plan and your eligibility for benefits. In most cases, these documents must be filed and made available to you by law.

- **Plan Document:** outlines the requirements to receive a pension.
- **Summary Plan Description**: a comprehensive summary of the above document.
- **Benefit Statement:** tells you if you have earned a right to a pension, and how much you would receive at retirement if you stopped work on the date of the statement.
- **Widows' and Widowers' Benefit Statement**: explains how much your benefit will be reduced to provide spouse protection.
- **Summary Annual Report:** briefly details your plan's investments.

You may also have participated in a 401(k) Plan, which allows you to invest money and defer taxes on the earnings until the money is withdrawn. The employer sets up the various investment vehicles and may supplement your contribution. You may also have participated in an Employee Stock Ownership Plan (ESOP). You will want to know the amounts due you and consider reinvestment of these funds with an advisor.

The Government: Social Security

Social Security is the system of social insurance set up in 1935 to prevent older people from falling below the poverty level. It was intended to supplement, not replace, the lost earnings of a retiree. It has become increasingly unrealistic to expect to live on Social Security payments alone. However, Social Security can improve your standard of living during retirement when combined with other income sources.

Below are Social Security facts to be aware of:

- You don't receive Social Security automatically, you must apply for benefits.

- Don't wait until the last minute to apply. If you are 62 or older and plan to retire, apply now. Apply 3 months before your 65th birthday, even if you do not plan to retire. If you apply later than the last day of the month you want benefits to begin, you may experience a delay in receiving your benefits.

- You will need to produce several documents to apply for benefits: your Social Security card; proof of age; marriage certificate, if applying for spouse or survivor benefits; and your last year's W-2 form. If you lack one of these documents, don't delay; your local Social Security office will tell you what documents can be substituted.

- It is advisable to periodically check your earnings record to see that your earnings have been "credited" by the Social Security Administration. (The agency has the proper forms for you to check this.) You receive one credit for every 3 months worked. The requirements for receiving benefits change periodically; consult your Social Security office for current eligibility requirements.

- Social Security is indexed to inflation through a Cost of Living Adjustment (COLA).

- Congress is gradually raising the age to receive full benefits, and is reducing even further the amount of benefits available at age 62.

- If you go over a certain threshold of earned income, your Social Security benefits may be reduced. The reduction formulas are changed periodically; consult your local Social Security office for up-to-date information.

Yourself: Savings, IRAs, Keoghs

There are a number of ways to add to your retirement income. When inflation was negligible, savings accounts were considered a safe way to earn a reasonable return. However, a savings account today may pay less interest than the rate of inflation, resulting in an actual decline in purchasing power; moreover, since savings account interest is taxed, the true yield may be even lower.

The Individual Retirement Account was created to allow individuals to set aside money and avoid taxation on the principal and interest until withdrawal in later years—when the individual would probably be in a lower tax bracket. Subsequent legislation has restricted some of the benefits of IRAs, such as the tax deductibility of the principal. An advisor can be useful in setting up the IRA, choosing the investments into which the money can be channeled, and in keeping you abreast of changes in the tax laws.

A Keogh plan is for self-employed people. These plans can be affected by changes in tax laws and there are penalties for withdrawing the money before reaching 59 and a half years of age. Because of this, these plans should be constantly monitored.

Investments

Investments can provide a source of income while helping you preserve or grow capital. As a retiree, you will probably have different investment goals than someone just starting out with a career and a family; generally, the younger person can take more risks in seeking growth of capital, while most retirees aim to preserve capital and minimize risks. At retirement, you need to review your investment goals (on your own or with a financial planner) to arrive at the right combination of investments for you. You'll want to consider the following questions.

- **Yield.** What is the yield and the probability of that yield continuing? Will the yield be reduced by commissions, fees and/or taxes?

- **Liquidity.** How quickly and easily can you convert the investment to cash? Are there penalties for doing this too early?

- **Safety.** Is this traditionally an investment that holds its value, or are there wide fluctuations? What events can cause these fluctuations? Is the investment insured or guaranteed? By whom?

- **Maturity dates.** If all your investments mature at once, will you have cash available when you need it? (Stagger maturity dates.)

- **Inflation.** How well does the value of your investment keep pace with inflation?

There are a wide range of investments available. These are best discussed with a competent financial advisor who has kept up-to-date with them.

Working

When deciding if and how much you will work in retirement, consider the long-term benefits and costs.

- You will be taxed on your earnings from your new job, and you will still be taxed for Social Security, even though you are collecting benefits.

- You may lose some of your Social Security benefits if your retirement income from work exceeds a prescribed amount.

- There may be benefits associated with working, such as health insurance.

- There are "indirect" costs of working, which include clothing, transportation and lunches out.

Income from Assets

You can sell items that are no longer useful to you or that would be more useful converted to cash, e.g., stamp or coin collections, furs, art, antiques, boat or piano. It is a good idea to have these items appraised if you are unsure of their current value.

Most retirees' major asset is their house, which has often appreciated significantly over the years. The sale of your house has many tax implications, which should be discussed with an advisor. In addition, a move from your home of several years involves more than a simple financial decision; it involves a thorough analysis of your present and future housing needs and your emotional attachment to your home.

Expenses

It is not possible to predict future expenses exactly, but it's important to make an informed estimate. The following breakdown is in descending order of importance in the average retiree's budget.

- **Housing.** Many retirees seek to reduce this cost by moving from a home which may now be too big (and expensive) for their needs. Taxes and maintenance costs may have been escalating with inflation. No longer tied to your job, you can now consider moving to a less expensive area or residence. However, you need to consider the costs and tax implications of selling a house and relocating. You may need to do some refurnishing in your new home; if moving to a rental apartment, consider the possibility of yearly rent increases; in condominiums or adult communities, maintenance fees can rise quickly.

- **Food.** Food costs can be controlled if you watch for sales and plan weekly menus. This is also an excellent time to cut down or eliminate purchases of non-nutritious or unhealthy foods.

- **Transportation.** This cost should go down as you are no longer commuting to work. If you have two cars, one may now suffice, especially if you live in, or are moving to, an area with good public transportation.

- **Medical care.** This is of major concern for older people. Probably the most effective way to avoid medical expense is to take the preventive approach—eat wisely and exercise regularly.

  Adequate health insurance is very important. What provision has been made by your employer to continue your health benefits? When will you be eligible for Medicare? Medicare alone may not be adequate; you may want to supplement it with some form of private insurance. Research you Medicare benefits carefully so that you know what it does and doesn't pay for.

  Research any supplemental insurance carefully for its comprehensiveness. For example, does it only cover expenses while in a hospital? (Many medical costs are not incurred in the hospital.) Does the insurance contain any provision for long-term care, which you may need later?

- **Clothing.** This expense may be reduced because you no longer need an expensive business wardrobe.

- **Leisure.** Because you'll have a lot more leisure time, these expenses will probably increase. However, you can control them by selecting activities that aren't too expensive or that offer discounts to seniors. Retirees are often able to travel during off-peak periods to receive the best possible fares.

- **Charitable contributions.** These need to be adjusted to your new budget. Your contribution might now be "the gift of time"; volunteering in the office of your favorite organization or helping it raise money can be more valuable than a direct monetary contribution.

- **Inflation.** An inflation rate of 6 percent erodes your purchasing power by 6 percent, so you must anticipate inflation as you would any other expense. (At 6 percent inflation, today's $100 item will cost $200 in only 12 years.)

More on Life Insurance

This is a good time to assess your current life insurance, which may not be suitable in your present situation.

For example, the policy you bought years ago may be unnecessary if your children are grown and your mortgage is paid off. On the other hand, a policy can be a good way of transferring wealth to children or grandchildren as an inheritance, and its cash value can be borrowed against. See your financial or insurance advisor to help you make the decision to continue or drop your life insurance.

Vital Papers

To help you plan your retirement finances and to ensure that you have the proper documents for any financial transaction, a complete inventory of all of your vital papers and their locations is essential.

If you have not been able to locate all your vital papers, the following information will be helpful.

- An official certificate of every birth, death, marriage, and divorce should be on file in the locality where the event occurred. The federal government does not maintain files or indexes of these records; they are filed permanently in a state Vital Statistics office, or in a city, county or other local government office.

- To obtain a certified copy of any document, write or go to the Vital Statistics office in the state or area where the event occurred. Addresses and phone numbers of City and State Department Records are listed in the telephone directory under Government offices.

To help you compile this list of vital papers and their locations, we've prepared a checklist.

A Parting Word About Finances

Well, it's not really a parting word. You'll be returning to this subject repeatedly throughout your retirement as you face decisions about insurance coverage, health care, travel and recreational expenditures, housing and relocation.

We hope this chapter has furnished you with enough information that you will take an informed approach to all these financial decisions, not the overconfident approach and not the "panic" approach. And we've also tried to point you toward additional resources that can answer your financial questions in more detail and help you arrive at a goal-oriented financial plan.

As you gather more and more information about your finances, your total financial picture will become clearer, your planning more focused. Proper financial planning alone is not sufficient to guarantee a satisfying retirement, but it is a necessary requirement for attaining peace of mind and achieving many of your goals in other areas.

Checklist of Vital Papers

List your important papers and their locations. Make sure that the people who are closest to you have copies of this list.

DOCUMENT	LOCATION
Birth Certificate	
Marriage Certificate	
Military Records	
Naturalization Papers	
Mortgage Records	
Deeds to Property	
Stock & Bond Certificates	

DOCUMENT	LOCATION
Owner's Title Insurance	
Automobile Title(s)	
Insurance Certification:	
Life	
Auto	
Home	
Health/Accident	
Pension Plan Information	
Social Security Records	
Income Tax Returns	
Receipts of Tax Payments	
Wills	
Trust Accounts	
Safe Deposit Box Keys	
Safe Deposit Box Contents	

Your Health: Wealth is Useless Without It

3

Questions to Ask Yourself

1. At my last medical checkup, was my blood pressure normal and my weight acceptable for someone of my sex and height?

2. Is my diet low in salt, fats and sugar?

3. Do I exercise several times a week?

4. Do I refrain from smoking and excessive use of alcohol?

5. Do I refrain from overeating?

6. Am I aware of the stresses in my life? Do I consciously try to avoid them or take steps to counteract their effect on me?

7. Can I climb a flight of stairs or walk briskly for a short distance without getting out of breath?

Many younger people can't answer many of these questions affirmatively, so don't be alarmed if you can't either. And as we get older, it takes more planning and effort to stay in good physical shape. (We told you retirement was a challenge!)

The good news is that as a retiree, you will have more time available to pursue fitness and health goals. With 10-12 extra hours per day which used to be taken up by work-related activities, you have no excuses such as "there's just not enough time to exercise" or "the food in the company cafeteria is not exactly the diet of Olympic champions."

Moreover, staying fit and healthy is a major prerequisite for accomplishing your other retirement goals. As many eagerly-anticipated retirements have been ruined by lack of health as they have for lack of funds. You may have lots of money for and interest in travel, but if you have difficulty walking, you're not going to hike up the Matterhorn or even stroll around New York City. Poor health can also force you out of your desired housing into accommodations where you receive needed assistance in daily functioning.

The three main areas in which you have control over your health during retirement are diet, exercise and stress. Let's look at each area to see what you can do.

Diet and Nutrition

Every few hours (and for some of us even more frequently), you put food into your mouth. Your decisions as to what goes in have major positive and negative effects on your health, particularly as you age. Diet has been identified as a major factor in preventing or complicating heart attacks, high blood pressure and other critical illnesses.

Perhaps your habits are already good, but only need a little fine-tuning. Great! But if you're like most of us, some of your habits could use some major tuning. Don't try to do this all at once. Cutting out all your favorite "treats" at once will probably be too stressful and only result in a "relapse" in a few weeks. It's much better to reduce or eliminate one type of food at a time. Once you've solidified a new baseline habit for that food, you can move on to another.

Consult a doctor or dietitian before making any major changes in your diet. If a health professional recommends particular changes, here are a few general guidelines for achieving them.

Reduce fat

- For protein, eat more fruit, vegetables, fish, poultry (without the skin), dry beans, and peas.
- Eat leaner cuts of red meat and trim off excess fat.
- Eat a moderate amount of whole eggs (two or three per week).
- Drink skim and low-fat milk.
- Limit intake of butter and cream; use polyunsaturated margarine.
- Broil, bake, boil, steam or roast foods, rather than fry them; use a rack when possible.

Reduce sodium

- Cook without salt; don't salt food after serving.
- Season food with lemon, spices and herbs, instead of salt.
- Learn to enjoy the unsalted flavors of food.
- Limit intake of salty foods: canned soups; potato chips; pretzels; salted nuts; popcorn; cheese; pickled foods; cured meats; and condiments, such as soy sauce, steak sauce, barbecue sauce, catsup, and garlic salt.
- Eat unsalted snacks: nuts, fresh fruit and vegetables.
- Check ingredients for salt and monosodium glutamate, and avoid products containing high levels of either.

Reduce sugar

- Use less of all sugars (white, brown, raw), honey and syrups in your recipes.
- For snacks, eat fresh vegetables, fruit, plain yogurt and whole-grain crackers, rather than candy, ice cream, cakes and cookies.
- Drink fruit juices and water, instead of soft drinks.
- Use no sugar in tea and coffee.

- Eat fresh fruit or fruits canned in their own juice, not in heavy syrup.

Why is it so difficult for many of us to institute these changes in our diet? Number one, many of the foods which are "bad" for us are very satisfying. Number two, we are often trying to change the habits of a lifetime. Number three, we often don't make the connection between these foods and our health and vitality. As you make gradual changes in your diet, you will find that you are developing newer, healthier habits. The healthier foods you have substituted may come to be just as satisfying as the "bad" old ones, particularly as you come to associate them with the increased energy and improved health you are experiencing as a result.

Exercise

You don't have to become some sort of "super-senior" to experience the benefits of exercise. We all read about 60-year-old triathlon winners or 80-year-olds completing their third marathon in a year. But for most of us, this is not only unrealistic but also undesirable, especially if we have spent many years being sedentary.

For most retirees, a moderate exercise program is "just what the doctor ordered." It's more pleasant, less grueling, and there's less risk of injury than the extremes of training for peak performance in major athletic events. No one ever got fitter by walking around on crutches. There are three basic types of exercise. Ideally, you should incorporate all three into your exercise program. Your doctor can help you decide on the best and safest exercise regime.

- **Aerobic/Endurance.** Typefied by running and aerobics
- **Flexibility/Stretching.** Typefied by yoga and calisthenics/warm-up exercises
- **Strength building.** Typefied by weight lifting and use of weight machines

You can build exercise into your normal daily activities by walking or biking rather than driving, picking a parking spot a little further from your destination, or taking the stairs instead of the elevator for short climbs.

Benefits

Exercise can benefit both your physical and your mental health in important ways.

- **Strengthens your heart, lungs and muscles.** The heart's ability to pump declines 8 percent for each adult decade; you use 50 percent less oxygen at age 75 than you do at age 25; the average adult loses 3-5 percent of his or her muscle tissue each adult decade. Exercise lessens this natural deterioration.
- **Increases flexibility.** Exercise keeps bones and joints from stiffening.
- **Curbs appetite.** Many people find they are actually less hungry after exercise.
- **Relieves stress and anxiety.** Exercise gives many people a physical release from pent-up emotional stresses.
- **Induces sleep.** Pleasantly tiring physical activity can help you sleep better than when you had no exercise.
- **Stimulates mental responses.** Physical health and mental alertness go hand in hand.
- **Improves physical appearance.** Exercise will help you stay slim and keep good muscle tone.
- **Creates a sense of well-being.** Looking and feeling good improves a person's outlook on life.

Stress

"Stress? What's that got to do with retirement?" A lot.

While you may be giving up a lot of the stresses of the workplace (commuting to work during rush hour, dealing with deadlines and demanding bosses and customers), retirement can bring on its own stresses unless you are prepared to deal with them.

In fact, two of the pioneering researchers on stress, Professors Holmes and Rahe, identified retirement as a major life stressor. Not as high on the scale as having one's partner die or being imprisoned for a major crime, but higher than having a child, major change in the health of a family member, or the death of a close friend.

That's not surprising when you consider that for many working people, retirement means a giving up of one's primary identity in society, the severing of ties with many friends and colleagues, major financial adjustments and a total revamping of their daily schedule and huge blocks of unstructured time to fill. Let's take a look at some of the stressors you may have left, as well as some of the stressors you may encounter by retiring.

Identifying Your Stressors

While you were working, you were subject to a number of stressors; in retirement, you will be able to minimize or avoid some of them. On the other hand, retirement can subject you to new stressors which you haven't had to manage before. The action of retirement, itself, has been identified as an important life stress on the Holmes Rahe Stress Evaluation Scale.

Some common stressors that can be avoided or minimized in retirement:

- Daily rush hour commute
- Juggling work and family life
- Business travel
- Scheduling vacation around a work schedule
- Running most errands evenings or weekends

- Tight work deadlines
- Not enough time for enjoyable activities, or needing to schedule them during peak usage periods
- Conflicts and disagreeable people at work

Some stressors frequently encountered in retirement:

- Need to monitor expenses more closely
- Large blocks of unstructured time
- Loss of identity as a corporate employee
- Relatives' demands on time
- Concerns about or actual physical deterioration or illness
- Loss of network of friends from work

Methods for Reducing Stress

There are ways to reduce stress; some steps you can take are described below.

- **Eliminate distorted or irrational thinking.** An example of this would be the belief that because you are about to retire, no one cares about you anymore or that you're over the hill.

- **Analyze recurring sources of stress** to determine how you can "break the cycle." This is easier in retirement, when you have more control over your schedule.

- **Plan for inevitable future changes,** like retirement. You will be better prepared for the actual event when it takes place.

- **Get regular exercise.** This releases pent-up anxiety and strengthens the body against stress.

- **Get enough sleep.** A rested body and mind can better handle stress.

- **Follow a well-balanced, nutritious diet.** This strengthens the body to better handle stress. A poor or unbalanced diet may actually stress the body.

- **Use relaxation techniques.** Progressive relaxation, meditation and yoga are just a few. There are many simple techniques that relax the body and mind in just a minute or two. You can also purchase relaxation tapes created for this purpose.

- **Adopt a less stressful schedule.** It is often possible to travel, do your banking and shopping and pursue other activities during the less frenetic "off-peak" hours.

- **Plan enjoyable activities.** These increase positive stress and decrease negative stress. Now that you're not working, you have more time for these activities.

- **Avoid situations/people that stress you.** You no longer have to deal with disagreeable work situations or colleagues, and you can determine the situations and people you encounter socially.

- **Talk to people about your problems.** This frequently relieves stress, and you may gain new perspectives that lead to creative new solutions.

- **Stop striving for perfection.** People who have unrealistic expectations of their own performance subject themselves to tremendous pressure. Retirement offers the perfect opportunity to go easier on yourself, focus less on achieving perfect results and more on the enjoyment of whatever you choose to pursue.

While you were working, you had fewer choices about dealing with many of your stressors; after all you couldn't totally avoid difficult people and situations; they were often part of the job. But in retirement, you have more control over the stressors in your life. You can avoid stressful people and situations; you can allow yourself to take the extra time you need to go a little slower.

Exercise 3 helps you identify former stresses and how to avoid them in retirement. But retirement may create some new stresses (e.g., too much time on your hands, financial worries); in Exercise 4, you will list these retirement stresses and formulate plans for managing them.

Exercise 3. Former Stresses I Can Avoid in Retirement

In the left-hand column, list your major pre-retirement stressors. In the right-hand column, write how you plan to manage your reaction to, or avoid, each stressor.

Pre-retirement Stressor	How to Manage or Avoid
1.	
2.	
3.	
4.	
5.	

Exercise 4. Retirement Stresses: Plans for Managing

In the left-hand column, list your anticipated stressors in retirement. In the right-hand column write how you plan to manage your reaction to each stressor.

Retirement Stressor	How to Manage
1.	
2.	
3.	
4.	
5.	

Health Care Legislation

It is extremely important for retirees to be up-to-date on the latest health care legislation, which is constantly under revision. Health legislation may undergo significant modification, or even be revised, from one year to the next.

You can keep abreast by contacting your Congressional representatives and the various government and civic organizations that deal with Medicare and the Aging and by reading newspaper and magazine articles on these subjects. Particular points of interest:

- Extent of hospital care benefits (number of days and deductibles)
- Extent of physician care and amount of coverage and deductibles
- Extent of coverage for prescription drugs and deductibles
- Extent of skilled nursing home care, home health care, hospice care
- Amount of tax surcharge you may have to pay as a Medicare enrollee

You have a choice. Your retirement can be a time when you passively watch your health slowly deteriorate. Or you can proactively manage your diet, exercise and stress levels so that you maintain optimum health for many years. Come to think of it, do you really have a choice?

To help you achieve the obvious choice of maximum health, we've included a Health and Fitness Action Plan, which will help you structure your own customized actions steps to insure a healthy retirement.

Exercise 5. Your Health and Fitness Plan

Fill in the blank spaces under A, B, C and D to reflect the steps you'll take to achieve optimum health and fitness.

A. Nutrition

1. Unhealthy foods I need to eliminate:

2. Healthy foods I need to eat more of:

3. Other steps I can take:

B. Exercise

1. Positive steps I can take:

2. Five new exercises/sports of interest to me that are consistent with my lifestyle:

C. Stress

1. My stressors (be as specific as possible; rather than just listing "work," specify which aspect of work):

2. My stress symptoms:

3. How I have coped successfully with my stressors:

4. Stressors I will likely encounter in retirement and how I plan to deal with them:

Stressor	**Coping Strategy**

D. Habits and Dependencies

Bad health habits I have and specific steps to eliminate them:

Habit/Dependency	**Steps to Eliminate**

What Will You Do With All That Time?

4

Questions to Ask Yourself

1. When confronted with a large block of free time, do I generally structure it well?
2. Do I know what kind of activities I enjoy, and do I set aside the time to participate in them?
3. Do I know and plan how to minimize time spent in boring or unpleasant activities?
4. Do I set priorities for myself and spend most of my time accomplishing those priorities?
5. Do I know what I will do during the large block of time previously taken up by work?

Ah, retirement! Ah, freedom from structured, rigid schedules. You can be anyplace you want to be at any time of day or night. Sounds like paradise, doesn't it?

But surprisingly, a lot of people find themselves using time poorly during retirement. They find that without the structure of work, they are unable to structure their own time. They wind up watching too much TV, or get roped into activities by others simply because "there's nothing better to do." They find they are spending time with people whose company they don't particularly enjoy. Or they may find other people making excessive demands on their time; after all, they're retired, aren't they?

While you may enjoy your spouse's or friends' company, there is no reason why you should have to accompany them to every activity, particularly those you don't enjoy. And while you may love your grandchildren, you may begin to resent it if your son or daughter simply assumes that now you will be available for unlimited child care.

Like money and health, time is a precious resource. Unlike money and health, everyone is allotted the same amount. Your challenge in retirement is to reclaim the time that up till now has been taken up by work, to prioritize your goals during retirement and to structure your time so you meet those goals. Good time management is a useful skill not just in business but also for your "third half of life."

Satisfiers/Dissatisfiers

To insure a satisfying retirement, you've first got to identify the types of activities that are satisfying and those that are dissatisfying. To structure your time, include as many satisfying activities as possible and as few dissatisfying ones as possible.

For instance, if you've always enjoyed telephone contact with many types of people, you may want to involve yourself with telephone fund raisers: avoid detailed paperwork if you've found it boring. Satisfying activities could be found through volunteer or leisure pursuits or paid employment. If you've always been a leader at work, you may want to seek out leadership positions during retirement; more typical "leisure" or volunteer activities may seem not dynamic or goal-oriented enough.

The Satisfiers and Dissatisfiers exercise will help you analyze your satisfiers, which indicate needs and interests. After you retire, writing your satisfiers/dissatisfier every six months or so will help you to revise your activities as necessary.

Your schedule will change dramatically in retirement. Below is a typical weekday before retirement. If 12 hours for work-related activities seems a little high, remember that this includes getting ready for work, coming to and from work, work brought home from the office and time spent talking about work. When you think about it, 12 hours is actually a low estimate for many of us!

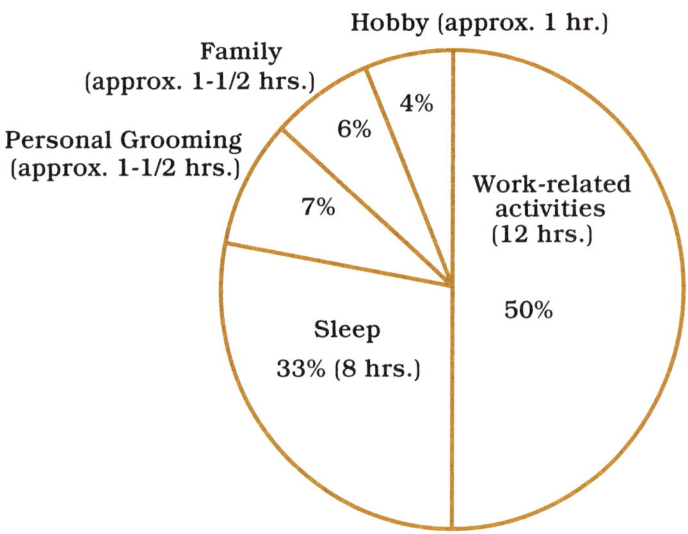

Figure 6 Typical Weekly Schedule Before Retirement

As you can see, a working person's time is usually highly structured with very little "free" time. One of the greatest challenges in retirement is the sudden "gift" of 12 hours additional free time—many people don't know what to do with it.

Because you will be faced with a much larger block of unstructured time in retirement, we have included some exercises to help you plan and manage it. As you complete the exercises, refer back to your satisfiers and dissatisfiers: do your time pies and schedules reflect your satisfiers?

Your Retirement Time Pies, which follow, ask you to consult two daily schedules (your time pies) for before and after retirement; the next exercise takes you one step further as you map out an ideal weekly schedule.

Including Your Partner or Spouse

When planning how you'll spend your time in retirement, it's good to consult your partner or spouse; in fact, the partner may want to complete the time pies and schedules also. See how closely your "ideal" schedules match. Perhaps one of you projected more time together than the other, who wanted more time alone or in separate activities. Perhaps your partner has an objection to you planning three games of golf per week, or to being included in an overambitious social schedule.

Most couples find that a little friendly exchange of ideas and negotiation upfront eliminates a lot of misunderstanding later. What's most important is your claim on your own time—you've worked many years for it, and you deserve it. While some compromise with family members is advisable and necessary, your main goal should be to prioritize and structure your time so your retirement calendar is filled with pleasant, rewarding activities.

Exercise 6: Satisfiers and Dissatisfiers

In the space below, make a list of some of the more important or time-consuming activities in your life. Consider what you've done at home, with family or friends, in the community or professional organizations, and in recent jobs.

Then, describe what you found satisfying about each activity/job and what you didn't like.

ACTIVITY: ____________________________

Satisfiers	Dissatisfiers
1. ____________________	1. ____________________
2. ____________________	2. ____________________
3. ____________________	3. ____________________
4. ____________________	4. ____________________
5. ____________________	5. ____________________

ACTIVITY: ____________________________

Satisfiers	Dissatisfiers
1. ____________________	1. ____________________
2. ____________________	2. ____________________
3. ____________________	3. ____________________
4. ____________________	4. ____________________
5. ____________________	5. ____________________

ACTIVITY: ______________________________

Satisfiers	Dissatisfiers
1. ______________________	1. ______________________
2. ______________________	2. ______________________
3. ______________________	3. ______________________
4. ______________________	4. ______________________
5. ______________________	5. ______________________

ACTIVITY: ______________________________

Satisfiers	Dissatisfiers
1. ______________________	1. ______________________
2. ______________________	2. ______________________
3. ______________________	3. ______________________
4. ______________________	4. ______________________
5. ______________________	5. ______________________

In the space below, list the common themes or patterns that you see repeated in your lists.

Satisfiers	Dissatisfiers
1. ______________________	1. ______________________
2. ______________________	2. ______________________
3. ______________________	3. ______________________
4. ______________________	4. ______________________
5. ______________________	5. ______________________
6. ______________________	6. ______________________
7. ______________________	7. ______________________
8. ______________________	8. ______________________
9. ______________________	9. ______________________
10. ______________________	10. ______________________

It is important to see where you are today in terms of your time management. In the space below, construct a time pie of a typical day before retirement. (Use the personal time-planning pie which appears earlier as an example.) Classify your activities any way you wish. Consider the percentage of your time committed to work-related activities; you'll need to replace those hours soon. At this point, you needn't be overly precise; rather, strive for general guidelines and preliminary planning ideas.

Compare your chart with that of your spouse/partner, and discuss how your respective time allocations overlap and affect each other.

Figure 7 Pre-retirement Time Pie

Now complete another time pie showing your hoped-for activities on a typical day after retirement.

Figure 8 Post-retirement Time Pie

Exercise 7. Retirement Time Chart

Fill in the chart to represent a typical week of your retirement. See how creatively you have replaced the 60-hour work week. If participating with a spouse/partner, consider the amount of time you will now be spending together and apart, and how closely you agree with this schedule.

	Mon.	Tues.	Wed.	Thurs.	Fri.	Sat.	Sun.
8:00							
9:00							
10:00							
11:00							
12:00							
1:00							
2:00							
3:00							
4:00							
5:00							
6:00							
7:00							
8:00							
9:00							
10:00							
11:00							

5 To Work or Not to Work?

Questions to Ask Yourself

1. Do I feel unproductive if I'm not working for pay?

2. Do I like to be part of a work team?

3. Do I need to supplement my income during retirement?

4. Have I always wanted to pursue a second career different than my first one?

5. Do I enjoy the routine of working, including preparing for and going to work?

6. As a retiree, will I miss my status as an employee of an organization?

7. Will I need contact with the workplace to keep up with developments in my field?

What? *Work* during retirement? In the "old" retirement model, the word "work" was about as welcome as a kryptonite collection in Superman's den. Work was what people retired from and avoided like the plague once they walked out the door of their former full-time employer.

But in the "new" retirement model, work is often very much a part of the equation. This is due to a number of factors:

- There may be an economic need to work in retirement, even for well-compensated individuals, because of inflation and earlier, longer retirements.

- Because people are retiring healthier and at earlier ages, they often have more drive and energy than the retirees of a generation ago. They continue to seek new challenges and opportunities to use old skills and learn new ones.

- Many people take advantage of retirement to pursue the lifelong dream of a second career or starting a business.

- There's a growing acceptance of older employees in the workplace and the realization that these older employees frequently have personality traits and skills which younger workers do not. Some organizations specifically recruit older workers because of their reliability, maturity, work ethic, experience and willingness to serve as trainers and role models for younger workers.

- Many retirees work largely for social reasons. They miss the built-in camaraderie of the workplace and the sense of being "intouch" with the rest of the world.

- Still others feel the need to work full-time or part-time to add structure to their day and purpose to their lives. For some people continuing to receive a paycheck is a measure of their effectiveness; the financial reward is a symbol that they are making a worthwhile contribution to the community.

So, are you going to work for pay or aren't you? Full-time, part-time, temporary, seasonal, consulting? Would you like to turn a long cherished hobby into a small business? Or would you prefer to have any "work" you perform during retirement be on a volunteer basis?

The answer lies in your own needs and motivations; no one else can answer it for you. But you can also take heart because your initial decision is not irrevocable. Many people have started their retirements pursuing nothing but leisure, but soon decided that they wanted to work part-time, which led to a full-time position. And many who said they would never "really" retire by ceasing to work for pay have found that the economic and social rewards of working were not great enough to compensate for the loss of freedom. So they quit! (Again!)

Following is a checklist which can help you assess what you might want from a job during your retirement. It can help you pick out the right type of job for yourself, or could help you make the decision that you really don't want to work for pay at all.

What Do You Want in a Job During Retirement?

You are not the same person you were when you chose your first job; your retirement job will be based on your current goals and values, not those of 30 or 40 years ago. The following exercise will help you analyze your current career goals and values. The three "priority items" should be your primary criteria for any work you do in retirement.

Check off each item that applies to you; then, prioritize the top three.

_____ A change from my original career

_____ A flexible schedule

_____ A career that relates to my retirement leisure goals (e.g., travel, writing, hobbies)

_____ Less stress

_____ Freedom from bureaucratic rules and layers of authority

_____ Something to help structure my retirement

_____ Increased income

_____ Something that builds on my original career

_____ A congenial atmosphere; pleasant group of colleagues

_____ Opportunity to "run my own show"

_____ Fewer responsibilities

_____ More/expanded responsibilities

_____ Increased status/prestige

_____ Opportunity to teach others what I know

After completing this exercise, you may decide that you have a definite desire to work, or you may decide you want the "traditional" retirement where that four-letter word doesn't bother to show its face. Or you may conclude that regardless of your desires, working may be an economic necessity.

Does it Pay to Work?

The question is, does it really pay to work during retirement? At first glance, that seems a silly question. After all, extra income is always welcome at any age. However, there are some additional considerations.

- You will pay taxes on any earnings.

- Once your earnings rise above a certain level, you will receive less Social Security. (Consult your Social Security office for most recent guidelines.)

- There are indirect expenses associated with work, including business clothing, meals, office "collections," gifts and parties, transportation to and from work.

Often, when you add up all the costs of working, they're not worth the economic benefit. However, there can also be some indirect financial benefits such as health and life insurance, employee discounts, or the use of company health and recreational facilities.

Let's take a closer look at the different types of employment. Most retirees don't want a full-time career; their second careers generally involve temporary, part-time and seasonal employment. For those who prefer self-employment, consulting or a small business are the most common options.

Temporary Work

Temporary work is growing in popularity because it offers so many benefits to both employers and potential employees.

- **Convenience.** Companies achieve greater staffing flexibility; temporary employees achieve lifestyle and schedule flexibility (daily, weekly, monthly). Some temporary employment firms are nationwide: it is possible to work for the same agency if you summer in one location and spend the winter in another.

- **Potential for permanent employment.** Temporary work often leads to permanent part-time or full-time jobs. Temporary work can provide a preview of many employers and fields and a chance to update skills.

- **Opportunity.** Over 90 percent of large U.S. companies now employ temporary workers. In 1982, temporary agencies referred 400,000 workers; in 1987, they referred 1,000,000; in 1989, they assigned 1,031,500.

Below are occupations in which temporary positions are increasingly common:

Clerical
Accountant
Chemist
Computer programmer
Engineer
Financial analyst
Pharmacist
Doctor
Lawyer
Financial officer
"Temporary Executive"

Part-time Employment

Part-time employment has advantages and disadvantages; the advantages include:

- Flexibility of schedule
- Usually low stress/responsibility level
- Stability, affiliation
- Possible option of full-time work

The disadvantages include:

- Limited pay/benefits
- Generally lower-level positions
- Part-time workers may not be accepted as members of the "team"

Seasonal Employment

This includes Christmas rush and inventory time for retail, tax season for accounting and tax preparation firms and the warm months for outdoor work. The best thing about seasonal employment is once its over, it's over for the year. The full-timers have to keep plodding along, while trying to recover from all the excitement, but you are free to take a total vacation until next year.

Consulting

Consulting is the selling of one's expertise and advice. The catch here is you must have a specific skill to sell and the ability and desire to sell it. Most people who become successful consultants during retirement have a well-defined specialty with a specific market niche (often their former employer is their first client). And the typical consultant spends about 50 percent of his or her time marketing services and 50 percent of the time delivering them *after the consultancy is in full swing*. At the beginning, it's more like 90 percent marketing and 10 percent delivery. That's why people with some marketing experience do better at consulting than those who just have technical expertise.

If you have the technical expertise and the marketing perseverance, consulting does have many advantages. You have control over your own schedule and you can work as little as you want (although if you turn down too much work, you may be seen as unmotivated or "not really serious").

Conversely, you can work as much as you want, assuming you have marketed yourself well. Many consultants begin with a minimal investment, printing up some business cards and working out of their homes or a small office which may be shared with others. And once you get established, your daily fee will often be greater than your compensation as a full-time employee.

There are a number of books on the market about setting up a consulting practice; you can learn a lot and avoid many mistakes by studying them.

Starting Your Own Business

Many of us have dreamed of starting our own business. Rather than retire from work completely, some people decide to realize this dream during their retirement. The "traditional," stereotypical situation is the kindly grandfather type who builds wooden toys in his workshop and sells them out of a remodeled playroom.

However, not all retirement businesses are so pedestrian or quiet. Depending on your drive, energy level and economic resources, you may embark on a business venture which involves even more effort, risk and complexity that your former full-time position.

You will choose the form and scope of your business based on these and other factors. You can begin a business in a number of ways; each has its own pros and cons.

Starting a Business:

Pros

- Opportunity to be your own boss
- Potentially unlimited financial opportunity
- Energizing challenge of bringing an idea to fruition
- Autonomy in creating own schedule, operating methods, service approach

Cons

- Financial risks: loss of own savings
- Original idea often necessary for success
- No blueprint to follow
- Business starts from scratch, with no clients or reputation
- Lack of support systems; you perform all functions
- You are completely responsible; the buck stops with you

Buying an Existing Business:

Pros

- No original idea needed
- A history and track record exist from which projections can be made
- Customers, facility, employees (if any) and equipment already in place
- Better financing possibilities. Lenders have more confidence lending to an existing business than to a start-up; for smaller acquisitions, sellers may offer financing to the buyer in the form of a note

Cons

- You're adopting someone else's baby, not creating your own
- Time-consuming search for the right business to buy
- Difficulty in evaluating the business and validating the books, even with an accountant
- Current owner may be hiding liabilities or overstating income
- Product or service being sold may be on the wane due to new technology or market factors
- The building lease may not be renewable on favorable terms once you take over

Franchising:

Pros

- A well-known franchise provides a recognized name, trademark, business appearance and product
- History and track record are already in place
- Standardization of products and services
- Proven concepts, access to training approach or system

Cons

- You are locked into the franchise's products, suppliers, operating procedures, advertising methods and budget
- The franchisor may make exaggerated claims for your success

- It may be difficult to protect the franchise location
- You may be putting in very long hours but still feel like an employee, not a business owner, because of the necessity to strictly follow the franchisor's "system"

If you are serious about your own business, it is imperative that you read some books which increase your knowledge in this area. You will find this useful whether you are running a high-powered business or selling home-made crafts out of your basement.

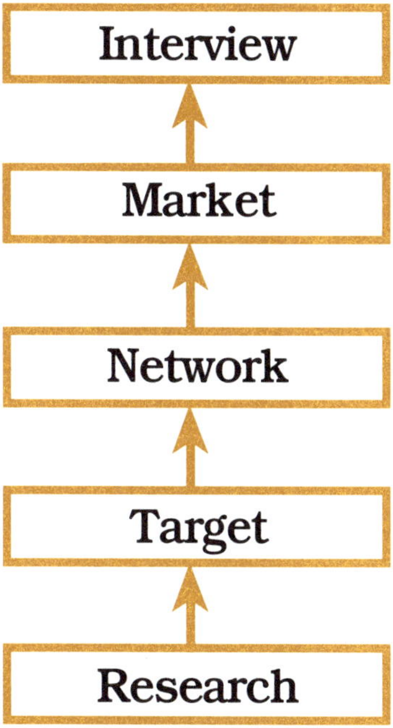

Figure 9 Steps in Finding a Job

Steps in Finding a Job

Let's say you've decided to confound the traditionalists and seek to work during your retirement. You may find this daunting because you haven't presented yourself to a new employer for many years. Whether you're searching for a full-time or part-time work, there is a sequence of steps to follow that will enhance your chances for success:

- **Research** the local job market (labor supply/company growth)
- **Target** employers who have specific needs you can fill as a mature worker
- **Network** at target companies
- **Market** yourself using resumés and cover letters
- **Interview** for actual positions

Researching and Targeting

Use printed publications to research and target part-time or temporary work and networking contacts to pinpoint:

- Fast-growth areas and industries
- Industries/employers with labor shortages or who mount visible recruitment efforts
- Industries/employers using many part-time employees or retirees
- Companies where you have a personal contact (could be a supplier to or a customer of your old company)
- Companies that have an urgent need for people with your skills
- Volunteer positions that might lead to a job
- Temporary agencies serving companies you've targeted (call the personnel director of a company that interests you and ask which temporary agencies they use)

Networking

Networking is the act of exchanging information with people you already know and obtaining information by getting referrals and introductions to new acquaintances.

The first step in networking is to develop a network list. Include everyone you know regardless of their apparent ability to provide you with job leads or other important retirement information. If the contact does not have this information, he or she may be able to refer you to someone who does. Eventually, you'll develop a comprehensive network list that will help you reach all of your retirement goals, whether or not they include working.

Resumés

A well-written resumé will be useful to an employer, as well as to yourself, by providing a summary of what you have to offer. There are two types of resumés; examples are provided on the following pages, and we have provided worksheets at the end of the section to help you create either type of resumé.

- **Chronological** resumés list your various positions in reverse order, latest first. Your accomplishments are highlighted within each position. The advantage of the chronological resumé is that it presents your background in a clear-cut, straightforward manner that enables the reader to quickly evaluate your experience.

- **Functional** resumés focus on your accomplishments in each functional or technical area, particularly the one in which you seek a job and "play down" your employment history; thus, you can draw attention away from work areas you do not wish to highlight and the sequence in which you progressed. This type of resumé is particularly useful when changing fields.

The chronological resumé is generally recommended, *except in the following situations:*

- Your employment history is erratic
- The job you seek requires a departure from your past history or experience
- You are attempting to return to a previous occupation

- You have an unusual combination of functional areas and/or skills and want to emphasize the breadth rather than the linear progression of your career.

Chronological

NAME
ADDRESS
PHONE NUMBERS

CAREER SUMMARY

Detail-oriented employee with over 20 years' experience in accounting functions of bookkeeping, inventory control, physical distribution, cost, accounts payable, and accounts receivable. Hands-on experience with various computer applications (mainframe and PC).

EXPERIENCE AND ACCOMPLISHMENTS

INTERNATIONAL BRAKE, Seattle, WA **1984 - Present**

A small firm manufacturing brakes and gear assemblies for railroad cars.

Inventory Accounting Clerk

Responsible for the posting of all inventory transactions, purchases, and shipments to ledger books.

- Provided the accounting supervisor with costs of individual items shipped, transferred, and consigned to customers. Received cash award for accuracy and reliability of performance.
- Generated monthly computerized cost of sales by creating own spreadsheet, using Lotus 1-2-3 software, resulting in time savings of 8 hours per month.
- Utilized IBM PC to compile monthly cost-of-sales figure, the first time this had been done by computer.
- Simplified and trimmed the amount and volume of paper-generated reports by creating new master forms.

T.J. BOWEN PRINTING CO., Seattle, WA **1977 - 1983**

A medium-size contract printer of magazines, paperbacks, and catalogs.

Inventory Clerk

Responsible for the posting of all inventory transactions to a cardex file.

- Converted manual inventory records to computerized printouts, resulting in a 50% time savings.
- Prepared material for entry into company computer for inventory.
- Stressed the need and importance of legible handwriting on production log cards to department heads, resulting in a 10% decrease in logging errors.

NORTHERN RAILROAD, Seattle, WA **1958 - 1977**

Interstate common carrier of commodities as defined by the I.C.C.

Accounting Clerk

Balancing of advanced and prepaid accounts, verification of car movement, checking accuracy of overcharge claims, and verification of voucher checks.

- Tracked and traced physical distribution using microfiche records.
- Saved company $20,000 by uncovering several questionable overcharge claims.

EDUCATION

AA, Seattle Community College, 1967. Major: Accounting

AAS, Seattle Community College, 1962. Major: Transportation

Functional

NAME
ADDRESS
PHONE NUMBERS

SUMMARY

Successful track record with a Fortune 500 corporation, including over 25 years of diverse staff and management positions. Extensive interfacing with highest levels of management, government, personnel, and public agencies. Special expertise in the following areas:

<u>Corporate Personnel Programs and Administration</u>
Employment
Management Development
Relocation
Equal Opportunity
Public Relations
Corporate Charitable Contributions

ACCOMPLISHMENTS

- Selected to assist the Chief Executive Officer in his Chairmanship of United Way of Southwest. Interfaced with top management of Fortune 500 companies while presenting an innovative solicitation program that resulted in new commitments from 31 companies. Assisted in implementing a unique sales training program for United Way personnel.

- Provided instruction on corporate personnel policies and practices to 3,000 managers during a 17-month period at Corporate Management Development Center.

- Established and managed the management development function for a newly formed division.

- Formulated corporate policy to geographically relocate 4,000 employees within the corporation; directed 12 divisional coordinators in implementing the relocation plan.

- Managed the personnel function of a major manufacturing facility. Administered programs in Recruiting and Employment, Equal Opportunity, Salary Administration, Benefits, Attitude Surveys. Successfully transferred 100 employees to facilitate operation phaseout.

- Interacted with Federal Government Auditors examining the corporation's compliance with Equal Opportunity regulations; received government recognition for total compliance.

NAME
Page Two

EXPERIENCE

Technology Unlimited, San Diego, CA 1964 - Present

Program Manager, Special Projects Office, Corporate Personnel 1988 - 1989

Manager of Communication, Special Projects, Corporate Personnel 1986 - 1988

Management Trainer, Management Development Center 1982 - 1986

Program Manager, Corporate Relocation Plan 1978 - 1982

Personnel Manager, East and West Coast Facilities 1970 - 1978

Senior Secretary/Personnel Specialist, Southwest Region 1964 - 1970

EDUCATION

Company-sponsored Management Education 1979 - 1989

New Manager School
Advanced Manager School
Career Development
Professional Staff Development
Personal Computer Systems
Management Behavior Theories
Effective Communication
Effective Presentations

AFFILIATIONS

American Personnel Association
American Society for Training and Development

COVER LETTER

Two-Column Matching Approach

Advertised Position

Part-time Accounting Head (20-25 hours) needed for small manufacturing company. Need experience with inventory control, accounts payable, accounts receivable, knowledge of PCs, mature, dependable. Write: Ms. G. Smith, Falcon Novelties, 123 Any Road, Pleasantville, WA 11111

==

Ms. G. Smith
Falcon Novelties
123 Any Road
Pleasantville, WA 11111

Dear Ms. Smith:

I possess excellent qualifications for your part-time Accounting Head. These include:

Your Requirements	**My Qualifications**
20-25 hours/week, small manufacturing company	Part-time is exactly the schedule I am seeking as I have just completed a 23-year accounting career, most recently with International Brakes, a large manufacturer.
Experience with inventory control, accounts payable, accounts receivable	Extensive experience in all these areas. Converted manual inventory records to computerized printouts, resulting in a 50% time saving at T.J. Bowen Printing.
Knowledge of PCs	Used IBM PC and Lotus 1-2-3 to develop computerized cost-of-sales figure at International Brake.
Mature, dependable	23-year career distinguished by excellent attendance and punctuality at three places of employment.

I will call you in a few days to further discuss the position.

Sincerely,

Mary Jones

Writing Cover Letters

You will make a stronger impact if you accompany your resumé with a cover letter tailored to fit the position. A good cover letter should address the employer's needs and how your experience meets those needs. A typical letter might cover the three areas mentioned below.

- **Your strengths.** Identify your skills, accomplishments and experience that match the employer's needs. To make this more dramatic, you could create two columns: "Company Requirements" and "My Qualifications."

- **Salary.** Many ads ask for "salary history" or "salary desired." A specific figure could eliminate you, being too high or too low; instead, you could list a fairly wide range, or you could write "salary requirements depend on job responsibilities and can be discussed at an interview."

- **Close.** Don't spend a lot of time writing the perfect closing to your letter: "My resumé is enclosed. I look forward to hearing from you" is fine. If a phone number is listed, say that you'll call in a few days to follow up.

Be persistent. If you have answered an ad, but received no reply, send another cover letter and include a copy of your previous letter and resumé. The employer may notice you the second time around. You can also follow up with a phone call; this is especially true if the ad is running every week.

Interview Tips for Retirees

You should use judgment when deciding whether to identify yourself as a retiree. For part-time jobs or for those which require "maturity" or experience, this can be an advantage. For other positions, you may choose not to mention your retiree status unless specifically asked. When interviewing for a job, people of retirement age may be asked questions related to concerns about their age. These questions may not be asked directly, but heard "between the lines." Below are likely employer concerns and tips on how to address them.

Your Health and Energy Level

Can you keep up with the pace of the job, or will you "fade out" at the end of the day or when the going gets tough? Will you call in sick and visit a doctor frequently?

How to Address:

Look and act your youngest and most energetic. Wear some bright colors for a youthful appearance, not all grays and browns. Answer questions with enthusiasm and show initiative by asking questions of your own. Emphasize recent accomplishments that took energy and perseverance. Stress your record of excellent health and attendance.

Your Dedication to the Job

Are you merely a leisure-oriented person seeking to "fill in a little time?" Will you take time off to be with grandchildren or attend club meetings? Was your financial package so good that you'll quit if the job gets too difficult?

How to Address:

Stress that although you accepted a package, you do not consider yourself retired; avoid any mention of the size of your financial package. Emphasize that you are still seeking new challenges, have always been a working person and want to use your skills and experience to help a new employer solve problems.

Currentness of Your Skills

This is a particular concern if you worked for one company for many years. Are you up-to-date on latest practices and technology, or are you hopelessly wedded to "the old way"? How quickly can you learn new skills?

How to Address:

Stress the many adaptations you had to make as your field changed; emphasize new technologies or procedures you learned at your company. Mention any training or night courses you've taken recently. Stress that you enjoy the challenge of learning new skills.

Your Adaptability

Can you adjust well to a new environment? Can you work and get along well with people of all ages and backgrounds?

How to Address:

Emphasize the changes to which you adjusted at former companies. Say that while you realize getting the work done is top priority, you consider getting along with co-workers equally important and that you've always been flexible and gotten along with people of all ages and backgrounds.

"Overqualification"

If you have a record of experience and responsibility, the employer may be concerned that you are overqualified for a position requiring less experience and responsibility.

How to Address:

Emphasize that your main goal at this point is to remain in the workforce and contribute your skills to an employer. State that you understand and accept that you may not have opportunities to use all of your skills.

Remember, the decision whether to work or how much is like all other retirement decisions—it's *yours* to make! Don't be distracted or swayed by what other people think is "right" or "appropriate." *You* drive the bus. Your decision should be based on your economic needs, energy level and psychological makeup.

Chronological Resumè Format

____________________Name
____________________Address
____________________City, State, Zip
____________________Telephone Number

POSITION OBJECTIVE

BACKGROUND SUMMARY

WORK EXPERIENCE

Company____________ Location (City, State)____________
Dates Employed________ Job Title____________
Responsibilities:____________

Accomplishments:____________

Company____________ Location (City, State)____________
Dates Employed________ Job Title____________
Responsibilities:____________

Accomplishments:____________

Company____________ Location (City, State)____________
Dates Employed________ Job Title____________
Responsibilities:____________

Accomplishments:____________

EDUCATION

School____________
Location (City, State)____________
Year of Graduation____________
Degree and Major Field____________
GPA, Activities, Organizations____________

Functional Resumé Format

______________________Name
______________________Address
______________________City, State, Zip
______________________Telephone Number

POSITION OBJECTIVE

BACKGROUND SUMMARY

MAJOR ACCOMPLISHMENTS

______________________(Function)

______________________(Function)

WORK EXPERIENCE

Company______________Location (City, State)______________
Dates Employed__________Job Title______________
Responsibilities:______________
Accomplishments:______________

Company______________Location (City, State)______________
Dates Employed__________Job Title______________
Responsibilities:______________
Accomplishments:______________

Company______________Location (City, State)______________
Dates Employed__________Job Title______________
Responsibilities:______________
Accomplishments:______________

EDUCATION

School______________Location (City, State)______________
Year of Graduation______________
Degree and Major Field______________
GPA, Activities, Organizations______________

6 The Leisure Smorgasbord

Questions to Ask Yourself

1. What leisure activities do I plan to pursue in retirement?

2. Would at least one of these activities require me to master a skill that involves lifelong learning?

3. Do these activities include group activities as well as solitary pursuits?

4. Have I already done some of my planned leisure activities, or am I just fantasizing that they might be rewarding or fun?

5. Have I included activities that can be done at all stages of my retirement—early, mid, and late?

A generation or two ago, "leisure" during retirement was limited to a few stereotypical activities considered appropriate to a person whose physical energy, mental acuity and stomach for challenge and adventure were all in precipitous decline. If the words "shuffleboard," "bingo," "knitting," or "escorted senior tour" all bring up aversive reactions similar to Maynard G. Krebs' to "work," don't worry. In recent years, an entire economic sector has grown up around the needs of today's younger, healthier retirees for stimulating, adventurous leisure activities. (And if you wish to knit or play bingo, these activities are still perfectly acceptable as well.)

In fact, one of your greatest challenges during retirement will be to develop comprehensive knowledge of the many activities that make up the "leisure smorgasbord," then to sort through these activities to determine which ones match your personal interests and energy level and finally to prioritize and pursue them.

Most retirees find that a balance of activities works best. While you may think that five games of golf per week is your definition of paradise, this may be a recipe for tedium, or even a lot of cursing and broken clubs. For most of us, too much of a good thing isn't good; variety in retirement can indeed be the "spice of life" and lack of it can produce a very bland meal. Lobster may be your favorite dish, but a plateful of it every day would be pretty boring if you had a 100-plate smorgasbord at your disposal.

It may seem paradoxical, but those retirees with an organized approach to leisure, perhaps even a "leisure plan," will find they are making optimum use of their leisure time and pursuing satisfying activities. Those who neglect this planning often find themselves at loose ends, either stir-crazy or bored. In planning your retirement leisure, you can't be too "leisurely"!

Let's take a look at just some of the activities you might choose to get involved in. Note that a lot of them would have been considered too demanding of a retiree a generation or two ago.

Leisure Activities in Retirement

SELF-DEVELOPMENT

Reading, study, seminars
Lectures, correspondence courses
On-campus courses
Writing
Library research
Researching your genealogy

FINANCES

Managing investments
Reading financial pages
Finance-related courses

FITNESS

Golf
Tennis
Bicycling
Swimming
Jogging, running
Walking, hiking
Other sports

SOCIAL ACTIVITIES

Large gatherings
Small groups
Entertaining at home
Family gatherings
Calling on friends
Visiting by phone

SERVICE ACTIVITIES

Civic groups
Church activities
Service clubs
Volunteer work

HOBBIES/PASTIMES

Arts, crafts
Collecting
Carpentry, home improvement
Gardening

AMUSEMENTS, RECREATION

TV, radio
Movies, theater, concerts
Dining out with others
Museums, art shows
Games, cards
Listening to music
Playing an instrument
Personal correspondence
Travel, vacations

Choosing Leisure Options

Confronted by such a vast array of activities, you may wonder how to choose between and prioritize them.

Of course, one key factor is enjoyment of an activity in the past. But you may not have had much time for leisure activities during your working life and there may be some activities you have never tried but would enjoy greatly.

Criteria for selecting leisure options include:

- What are your skills?
- What are your interests?
- Does this option match your health status and energy level? Will it continue to do so as you get older?
- Can this activity be a lifelong pursuit (mastering the violin) as opposed to a time-limited project with a definite end (painting the deck)?
- Does this option match your communication style and your need for group vs. solitary activities?
- Is this activity within your budget?

Keep in mind that it is you who determines the intensity and pace with which you pursue retirement leisure activities and goals. "Jogging and running" could mean anything from a 2-mile jaunt three or four times a week to stay in shape to a rigorous training schedule to prepare you for personal bests in competitive races.

Some Specific Leisure Options

There are several leisure options which have gained so much popularity for retirees in recent years that they are worthy of special mention. These include:

- Volunteering
- Returning to school
- Elderhostel/Interhostel

Volunteering

Many retirees report finding tremendous satisfaction in serving others or sharing their experience and skills. Volunteering can be categorized as follows:

- Community service
- Hospitals, social agencies, and charities
- Government programs
- Youth work
- Politics
- Business groups, such as National Executive Service Corps and Service Corps of Retired Executives

Is volunteering for you? A desire to help others is usually the basis for volunteer work. Other indicators of suitability are:

- Compassion for others who are in need, despite the little time you may have had to act upon these feelings in the past
- A deep interest in the social issues of the disadvantaged, e.g., elderly and disabled
- A need to develop and teach others (in your work you may have enjoyed training and teaching subordinates or co-workers)
- Great satisfaction from volunteer work in the past

Having realistic expectations of volunteer work is important. Volunteers may be disappointed if they forget that many organizations have full-time paid career professionals in key positions of management.

It may be presumptuous to think that as a volunteer you will immediately be assigned the more challenging and interesting tasks. However, the volunteer coordinator and others in the organization should be aware of your skills and experience. If you have particular skills in budgeting, fundraising, operations management, or other areas and wish to use these while volunteering, the volunteer coordinator should know about them. Your choice of volunteer agency will be based on their willingness to utilize your best skills in addition to your commitment to their causes, liking for the organization's culture and the people in it, convenience, scheduling and or other issues.

Back to School

Probably no other issue regarding leisure options in retirement has received more media attention than that of retirees returning to school. An astonishing number of the students on college campuses today are older adults. Colleges and universities have done much to encourage the trend, offering the following incentives:

- Tuition discounts for graduate and undergraduate courses

- Courses in which retirees are exempt from exams and grades to encourage retirees whose purpose is primarily enrichment

While some retirees clearly look forward to returning to the classroom, others are uncertain. Here are some indications that it might be right for you:

- An abiding eagerness to learn; a receptivity to instruction

- A desire to extend your knowledge of your own field or to explore other fields

- A desire to acquire a degree or credential you have long delayed.

  Although many retirees go back to school, some hesitate to do so because of insecurities; described below are three areas of insecurity.

- "I'm not as sharp or as flexible as I used to be. I'm having increasing trouble remembering names, dates and other information. (Research shows that there can be some short-term memory loss in later years, but for most people it would not be a barrier to doing well in class. Part of your so-called "memory loss" stems from the fact that you've been alive longer and have more dates, names and experiences to remember!)

- "I'd feel ignorant and at a disadvantage trying to compete with all those bright young minds." (Most schools and colleges offer refresher courses for those who have been away from the classroom for a long time. Besides, your pursuit of knowledge has a different flavor than that of a 20-year-old. He or she is preparing for a job; you are there for enrichment after a lifetime of working. Both you and your younger classmates will realize that direct comparisons and competition are not only useless, but irrelevant.)

- "What would I have in common with a teenager? I'll be like a fish out of water." (Most retirees who return to school discover that they are stimulated by the young, who are often very open to their experience and practical wisdom. Besides, the average age on campuses has become decidedly older!)

Elderhostel/Interhostel

One of the most interesting options, recently available, is the opportunity to combine travel and learning through the Elderhostel and Interhostel programs. These programs are intellectually stimulating and can be physically adventurous as well. They bear little resemblance to the stereotypical escorted tour group.

Elderhostel

Elderhostel is an educational program for older adults who want to continue to develop new interests and enthusiasms.

Elderhostel participants enjoy inexpensive, short-term academic programs at educational institutions around the world. The programs are available to adults age 60 and over and are at least a week long. The courses represent all areas of learning and interest and participants live in university dormitories. You may request to be put on a mailing list to receive descriptions of all future programs.

For more information, contact:

Elderhostel
75 Federal Street
Boston, MA 02110
(617) 426-7788

Interhostel

Interhostel offers the opportunity to travel abroad and learn about foreign cultures and people in more than 15 countries and 21 foreign regions. Each program, designed for adults over 50, lasts approximately 2 weeks and offers lectures, seminars, field trips and excursions. Activities are led by professors and experts from the region or country the participants are visiting and top quality accommodations are guaranteed.

For more information about Interhostel, contact:

Interhostel
University of New Hampshire
6 Garrison Avenue
Durham, NH 03824
(603) 862-1147

Leisure Options Resource List

The key to a fulfilling leisure schedule in retirement is *balance*. We would hate to see you either bored from inactivity, overdoing on one (formerly) pleasurable activity, or so overscheduled that your retirement is hectic and overstressed as you run from one "leisure" activity to another. The following resource list can help you expand your knowledge of available leisure and volunteer opportunities, and connect with those which match your skills and interests. After that, we've included a listing of printed materials which will also be useful. With all this information, you've got no excuses. Use your leisure time wisely and enjoy. You've earned it!

Organizations to Contact - Leisure Options Resource List

ACTION, 1100 Vermont Ave., N.W., Washington, DC 20525. (202) 634-9135. Includes:

VISTA (Volunteers in Service to America)

SCORE (Service Corps of Retired Executives), Small Business Adm., 1441 L Street N.W., Room 100, Washington, DC 20416

RSVP (Retired Senior Volunteers Program)

FGP (Foster Grandparents Program)

PEACE CORPS

AARP Volunteer Talent Bank, 1909 K Street, N.W., Washington, DC 20049. (202) 434-3219. Request a registration packet.

International Executive Service Corps, P.O. Box 10005, Stamford, CT 06904-2005. (203) 967-6000. Overseas volunteer assignments for retired executives.

Literacy Volunteers of America, 5795 Widewaters Parkway, Syracuse, NY 13214. (315) 445-8000. Helps adults increase literacy skills.

National Executive Service Corps, 257 Park Ave. South, New York, NY 10010. (212) 529-6660. Volunteer consulting for non-profits.

National Park Service, Office of Information, U.S. Dept. of the Interior, P.O. Box 37127, Washington, DC 20013-7127. (202) 208-6843. Volunteering in the national parks.

Senior Community Service Employment Program (SCSEP), American Association of Retired Persons, 601 E Street, N.W., Washington, DC 20036. (202) 434-2277.

Senior Environmental Employment Program (SEE), American Association of Retired Persons, 601 E Street, N.W., Washington, DC 20036. (202) 434-2277.

Service Corps of Retired Executives (SCORE). Volunteer assignments consulting to small business. Contact through your local small business administration office.

VITA (Volunteers in Technical Assistance), 1815 North Lynn Street, Suite 200, Arlington, VA 22209. (703) 276-1800. Provides volunteers to help in developing countries.

Local organizations to contact (check local phone book for addresses):

National Federation of Settlements and Neighborhood Centers
Boy and Girl Scouts
Boys Club
American Red Cross
Big Brothers/Big Sisters
United Way
Health and Welfare Council
Council of Social Agencies
Museums, hospitals, schools
Senior centers
Community centers
County Extension Service (rural areas)
YMCA/YWCA/YMHA
Your church or synagogue
Public Health or Welfare Dept.
American Cancer Society
Meals on Wheels

Educational Resources

College Level Examination Program, P.O. Box 6600, Princeton, NJ 08541-6600. (609) 951-1026.

Elderhostel, 75 Federal Street, Boston, MA 02110. Will send catalog describing their low-cost, short-term academic programs held in colleges and universities in fifty states, Canada, and abroad.

Institute of Lifetime Learning, AARP, 601 E Street, N.W., Washington, DC 20049. (202) 634-9135. Provides activity kits for mini-courses on a variety of topics.

Interhostel, University of New Hampshire, 6 Garrison Ave., Durham, NH 03824. (603) 862-1147. Offers education programs abroad for adults over age 50.

National University Continuing Education Association, One Dupont Circle, N.W., Suite 615, Washington, DC 20036. (202) 659-3130. For a list of member universities that offer independent study programs through extension services, call Peterson's Guides, (800) 225-0261.

National Home Study Council, 1601 18th Street, N.W., Washington, DC 20009. (202) 234-5100. Provides a free Directory of Accredited Home Study Schools.

Local organizations to contact (check local phone book for addresses):

Adult Education (through public schools)
Community centers
Community colleges
YMCA/YWCA/YMHA
Local colleges and universities

Printed Materials—Retirement Leisure

Books:
Leitner, Michael and Sara. *Leisure Enhancement.* Binghamton, NY: Haworth Press, 1989.

Moran, Joan M. *Leisure Activities for the Mature Adult.* Minneapolis, MN: Burgess, 1979.

Osgood, Nancy. *Leisure Life After Work.* New York: Praeger, 1982.

Redd, Robert O. *Achievers Never Quit — How to Create a Life Plan for the Years After Fifty.* Ada, MI: Thornapple Press, 1989.

Smaridge, Norah. *Choosing Your Retirement Hobby.* New York: Dodd, Mead & Co., 1976.

Pamphlets:

Elderhostel Catalogue. 75 Federal Street, Boston, MA 02110.

Elderhostel provides catalogues describing colleges, dates and course descriptions, all reasonably priced.

Interhostel Catalogue. University of New Hampshire, 6 Garrison Avenue, Durham, NH 03824. (603) 862-1147. Provides descriptions of upcoming programs, dates, prices.

References:

U.S. Government Printing Office, Washington, DC 20402. Lists publications on retirement and leisure activities.

Changing Roles/Relationships

7

Questions to Ask Yourself

1. How will my retirement affect the nature of my relationship with my family members, partner, or spouse?

2. How will household responsibilities and routines need to be readjusted?

3. What are the roles that will bring me the most satisfaction in retirement?

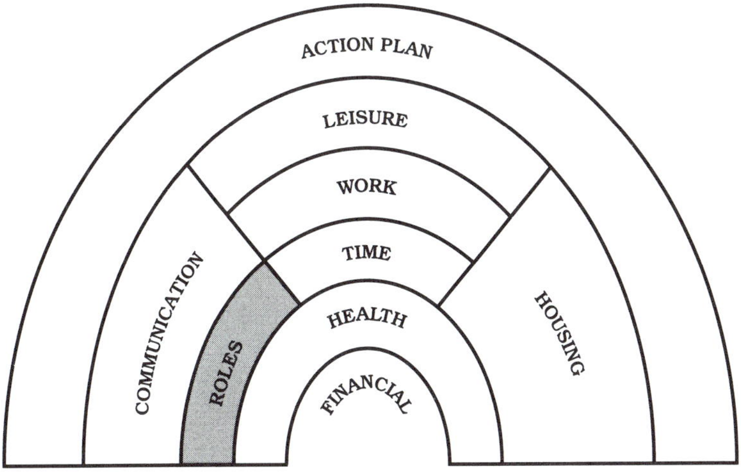

Figure 10 Building Your Retirement: The Retirement Arch

4. What are the roles I may want to limit or avoid?

5. Which relationships do I wish to deepen during retirement?

6. How do I plan to make new friends during retirement?

Retirement Means Major Role Changes

Roles are the behaviors or functions you assume with others, e.g., employee, parent, grandparent, mentor, friend and colleague. Retirement represents the major role change from "full-time employee" to "retired person." As a retired person, you now have the time and opportunity to choose roles for their ability to provide meaning and satisfaction; don't just "fall" into a role because it is what your parents or friends did in retirement.

How do you conceive of your roles during retirement? Grandparent and substitute child care person? Part-time worker and part-time golfer? Helpmate and companion to your partner? It's good to have a clear idea of your desired role so that others don't make this decision for you based on their needs and demands.

Relationships involve interaction with others within your roles. When you retire, relationships may be readjusted. When you were working, the workplace provided "ready-made" friendships; as a retiree, you will have to take more initiative to maintain and increase your network of friends.

You may need to modify or adapt various responsibilities you have assumed within your relationships, which may change the nature of them. Your responsibilities as partner or spouse will be affected as you'll probably spend a lot more time at home: you may have to renegotiate the division of household tasks and the amount of time you'll spend together and alone. You may also want to renegotiate your responsibilities to other family members and friends.

Relationships assume great importance in retirement. A study of 7,000 retirees found a positive correlation between longevity and adequate social contact. Initiating social relationships based on your individual interests can make the difference between an active, vibrant retirement and a listless, lonely one.

The case studies, appearing later, illustrate the challenges that retirees face regarding roles and relationships. Whether a case relates specifically to you or not, brainstorming solutions to it can help you find solutions to your own issues.

Planning Your Retirement Roles, Relationships and Activities

In planning the roles you will assume in retirement, a good first step is to analyze your pre-retirement roles. How meaningful are these roles now, and how will you adapt them to retirement? The case studies included here will help you arrive at these decisions.

In addition to prioritizing roles, it is helpful to prioritize your relationships: Who do you want to spend more time with? How often do you want to see them? Who do you want to spend less time with? What activities do you most enjoy doing with each person? The exercise Your Retirement Relationships will assist you in this area.

By integrating this group of exercises with earlier ones, you help to insure a meaningful, fulfilling retirement as satisfying roles, activities and relationships are pivotal to retirement satisfaction.

Redefining Your Relationships

The changes that you'd like to make in your roles and relationships may not match the expectations of those around you: your son may expect you to spend more time babysitting his children; your mother may assume that you will spend more time with her; your golf partner may

push you to play two extra rounds a week.
It is your responsibility to renegotiate and redefine your relationships to reach your own, not others', retirement goals. If you don't, you will find yourself stuck with roles and responsibilities you don't want and you'll have no one to blame but yourself.

Another aspect of redefining your relationships is forming new ones. You can find people with similar values and interests to your own by joining professional or social organizations and by networking with other retirees, former colleagues and other contacts in the community.

Tips for Retired Singles

There is an increasing number of retired single people. This is due to the increased divorce rate as well as increased life expectancy, with women tending to outlive men. Often, retiring from the full-time workplace can be a shock for a single person; he or she never realized how much of a social outlet work provided. Here are a few tips for the newly retired single.

- Living alone doesn't have to mean being lonely, but now that you are retired, you will have to make conscious, planned efforts to maintain and extend your social network.

- Maintain a varied, balanced social life. Make regular contact with those younger and older than you, not just people at your "age and stage."

- Don't depend on any one person to meet all your social/emotional needs.

- Volunteer or part-time work can be a social outlet.

- Join clubs or organizations where you can meet people who share your interests, concerns and values; serve on a committee.

- Join a support group. There are a number of groups

for older single people; some are specifically for widows and widowers. These can be found by reading the "Community" page of your local paper or contacting self-help clearinghouses or social agencies, community centers and religious organizations.

Roles and Relationships - Not to Be Taken Lightly!

Many people who have planned well in other areas such as finance find to their chagrin that they haven't planned the "people" areas of their retirement enough. They may find retirement lonely or unstimulating. Don't let this happen to you! This chapter has given you the tools to plan a retirement in which you live out your preferred roles (not someone else's preferred role for you) and spend time with people who are important to you.

Case Study I: Sylvia

At the time of her retirement, Sylvia, at 53, was a very well-paid salesperson at a computer corporation. Her job was to sell office automation systems to management consulting firms. She enjoyed the intellectual stimulation of dealing with top managers with good educations, controlling her own schedule and getting concrete feedback on her effectiveness. In her spare time she particularly enjoyed reading; remodeling and redesigning her home, which she did very competently; and playing with her grandchildren.

During retirement, she found that routine homemaking chores and errands, which bored her, were taking up most of her time. Some of these chores and errands were for her mother-in-law, who was quite capable of doing them for herself, but who seemed to enjoy the attention and companionship. At the suggestion of a friend, she joined a bridge club. She enjoyed the challenge of the game, but found that the other members did not share her other interests—she did not enjoy the 2-hour socializing that took place after the game.

1. How would you evaluate Sylvia's retirement satisfaction?

2. What roles and activities should Sylvia spend more or less time in to increase her happiness?

Case Study II: Jack and Lois

Jack has worked hard as a chemist for a pharmaceutical firm for the past 25 years; at 62, he is looking forward to retirement. He'd like to travel for 6 months, identifying a possible retirement relocation site.

His wife, Lois, is 56. She went back to work 8 years ago after many years as a full-time wife and mother to their four children.

Through a combination of hard work and some evening business courses, Lois worked her way up to the position of Office Manager in a medium-sized chain of real estate offices. She is now hoping for a Vice-Presidency.

Lois enjoys the responsibility, status, friends, money and independence that her career gives her. She isn't ready to retire yet, even though Jack is eager to begin his retirement with Lois. She does want to spend some time with Jack during his retirement, but not at the expense of her career.

Jack and Lois have agreed to discuss this matter next weekend.

1. What are the key issues that ought to be included in that discussion?

2. What are possible solutions and the corresponding consequences?

Case Study III: Frank and Linda

Frank and Linda are almost 60; they plan to retire when they are both 62. They have saved enough money to look forward to a comfortable retirement.

Frank was a human resource manager for an electronics company; Linda coordinated nationwide conferences for an accounting firm. Both have led somewhat separate lives due to travel pressures, relatively demanding careers and few shared leisure interests. Their leisure time has almost always been spent apart. Because of the time they've spent away from home, neither partner has developed extensive social contacts or activities in their community. Years ago, they enjoyed playing tennis with another couple, but they've since lost touch with them.

1. What are the issues that need to be identified and discussed?

2. What are some ways in which these issues could be resolved?

Case Study IV: Sally and Arthur

Sally is a homemaker and mother; her children are now grown. Arthur, her husband, was a successful manager who retired 6 months ago.

Because Arthur was so involved in his work, he developed few outside interests. He's been staying around the house a lot and getting underfoot; even worse, he's telling Sally how to manage their home and her life.

Tensions are mounting between them, and arguments over seemingly insignificant issues are increasing.

1. How can Arthur and Sally defuse the tension?

2. What can they do to reestablish harmony in their relationship?

Case Study V: Mark

Mark, who is in his late 50's, became a widower last year soon after his retirement.

He has two grown children who live out of town. While he has a range of interests, many of his activities were enjoyed with his late wife. Moreover, he and his wife were part of a social set with several other couples.

Although his friends still keep in touch, Mark is not invited out socially very often. When he does spend time with these couples, he feels like a "fifth wheel." He is aware that his friends are drawing away from him and he is feeling increasingly isolated.

1. What are the issues that Mark has to come to terms with?

____
____
____
____
____
____

2. What are some possible steps he can take to deal with his situation?

____
____
____
____
____
____

Case Study VI: Ralph

Ralph has always enjoyed being with his grandchildren and had planned to spend more time with them when he retired.

After he retired, his daughter got a part-time job. Her child care help has not always been reliable and lately his daughter has been calling Ralph several times a week, often at the last minute, to ask him to babysit.

Ralph has always agreed, but he has missed engagements that were important to him, including a golf lesson and a meeting with his accountant. He is beginning to worry that this pattern may continue or worsen.

1. Why has a formerly desirable role become uncomfortable for Ralph?

____
____
____
____
____
____

2. What can Ralph do or say to deal with this situation?

____
____
____
____
____
____

Exercise 8: Choosing Meaningful Retirement Roles

For many people retirement satisfaction is determined by the amount of time they spend in roles that they have chosen and how freely they are able to express themselves within those roles. Analyze where you are today using the chart that follows.

List the principal roles you are engaged in today at the far left on the next page. Consider everything you do at work (paid or volunteer) and in your family and community, social and religious activities, hobbies, and athletics.

In Column 1, rate how meaningful each role is to you

(use scale of 1-10, 10 being the most meaningful).
In Column 2, use one or two words to specifically describe how you feel in each role (e.g., fulfilled, excited, obligated).

In Column 3, indicate the amount of time you spend a week in the role. Use a plus (+) or minus (-) if you want to spend more or less time in the role during retirement.

Suggested Roles

Mother/Father
Spouse/Significant other
Son/Daughter
Companion
Niece/Nephew
Aunt/Uncle
Cousin
Sister/Brother
Neighbor

Supervisor
Classmate/Alumnus
Work colleague
Work positions (may be multiple)
Community member
Club member
Professional association member
Athletics club member
Hobbyist
Traveler
Reader
Gardener
Domestic roles (may be multiple)
Investor
Member of organized (or other) religion

YOUR RETIREMENT ROLES

	COLUMN 1 How meaningful?	COLUMN 2 How will you feel in this role?	COLUMN 3 Indicate how much time per week you now spend in this role. (Use **+** or **-** to indicate desired changes.)
1. ________ ROLE	________	________	________
2. ________ ROLE	________	________	________
3. ________ ROLE	________	________	________
4. ________ ROLE	________	________	________
5. ________ ROLE	________	________	________
6. ________ ROLE	________	________	________
7. ________ ROLE	________	________	________

Exercise 9: Your Retirement Relationships

Think ahead to your first few months of retirement. There will be much more time available to develop new friendships and strengthen old ones. Enter in Column 1, in the appropriate category, the people you will want to see. Then, list in Column 2 how often you would realistically expect to see them (O=Often; S=Sometimes; R=Rarely). In Column 3, list the activities you prefer to engage in with this person.

NAMES	FREQUENCY	ACTIVITIES
Family		
________	________________	______________________
________	________________	______________________
________	________________	______________________
________	________________	______________________
________	________________	______________________
Friends (old)		
________	________________	______________________
________	________________	______________________
________	________________	______________________
________	________________	______________________
________	________________	______________________
Friends (new)		
________	________________	______________________
________	________________	______________________
________	________________	______________________
________	________________	______________________
________	________________	______________________
Work Contacts		
________	________________	______________________
________	________________	______________________
________	________________	______________________
________	________________	______________________
________	________________	______________________

Other (neighbors, community members, etc.)

Look over your list. What conclusions can you draw? Is your support network in place? Do the people you've identified know that they are part of your plans? Write your comments below.

Your list should give you a fairly specific analysis of your probable social relationships in retirement based on your current social ties.

Below, write out the concrete steps that you can now take to prepare for a satisfactory social life.

8 To Move or Not to Move: Still Another Question

Questions to Ask Yourself

1. Do I feel "at home" in my community? (Do I like the people living there? Do I know many of my neighbors?)

2. Can I manage my current home's rent, mortgage, repair bills, taxes and other expenses on my retirement income?

3. Do I have the energy and/or help to maintain my house during retirement?

4. Is my home accessible to shopping, transportation, medical and social (and other necessary) services?

5. Does my house meet my requirements for space and lifestyle during retirement?

6. Do I find the climate where I live pleasant and suitable to my health or ability to care for myself?

Planning Your Retirement Housing

There are a lot of myths surrounding retirement, moving and housing. Probably one of the biggest is that it's a good idea or a common occurrence for someone to move out of their home of a lifetime the month after retiring. "You're retired! Chuck all your social contacts, support systems, familiar neighborhood and environment and head for Florida, Arizona, or Pago Pago!" (No one says where those already living in Florida, Arizona, or Pago Pago should head to.)

You have just undergone a major life stressor, retirement. To immediately add another major stressor such as a relocation would be foolhardy unless you have planned it for many years and have a full knowledge of and familiarity with the community you are moving to. For this reason, few retirees race off to the Sunbelt immediately after severing their ties with the company. A recent study by Retirement Advisors found that less than 20 percent of people 65 and older relocate to another state and that most retirement moves are within the same geographic area.

Any decision to relocate, even within your local area, must be carefully considered and planned, because it will have major implications on the other areas of the Retirement Arch and your goals in those areas. Do you or your partner plan to work and how will your relocation affect that decision? Do you need to be near a major population center? Children or other relatives? Do you need access to particular health care facilities or other community services? Will the relocation be financially advantageous, and what are some of the hidden costs?

The Key Variables

Any housing decision really involves three variables, all of which must be considered:

- Location: What city, state, or region will you live in?

- Residence: What type and size meets your needs? What

can you handle in terms of finances and maintenance?

- Living Arrangement: Will you live with your partner? Other family members? Alone? In some sort of community setting?

Three Stages of Retirement

Making your retirement housing decisions more complicated is the fact that there will probably be several of them. A generation or two ago, when people didn't live as long and retired later, one decision usually carried people through most of their retirement. But today, when you may be retired 25 or 30 years, you will be going through several stages of retirement, each with its own type of housing needs. These stages include:

- Active Stage. This stage comes early in your retirement; you can maintain your own home and provide for all or most of your own needs (transportation, medical services, recreational and community activities).

- "Slow Down" Stage. This comes at different ages for different people, but most of us will find that somewhere in the middle of our retirement, health problems may begin to curtail some of our day-to-day and recreational activities.

- Dependent Stage. In the later years, you may not be able to perform certain necessary daily functions yourself. You may need to live near supportive family members or in a group setting where these needs can be met by the facility itself or community or professional services. And if you are a female, you may need to plan on living without your partner for a number of years, since statistically, women live longer than men and are more likely to be living alone in the later years.

You should begin planning now for all three stages. That way, you'll have a back-up plan even if you remain independent and healthy for all or most of your retirement.

Recommended Research

The decision to relocate should only be made after careful analysis of financial, emotional and logistical factors. Any move should further the goals you have set in the other retirement areas.

- Know what you can afford in terms of both housing and living costs.
- Call/write for information to the local Chamber of Commerce, the Visitor's Bureau, the Real Estate Association, and other area resources.
- Call/write the state's Department of the Aging (c/o the Governor's office); in large cities, contact the local Department of the Aging (c/o the Mayor's office).
- Subscribe to local newspapers.
- Visit the community you are considering at different times (in and out of season if it is a resort area). Stay for a few weeks, or months, if possible.
- Talk to local people, especially retirees.
- Engage in normal day-to-day activities in the area under consideration.

Residential Alternatives

There are many residential alternatives, quite a few of which are listed below. A more complete list and description is in the Glossary of Housing Options for Older Americans at the end of the section. There are also innovative approaches to these alternatives, such as renting part of your house to a boarder. Informed decisions are based on facts, your feelings, common sense and good judgment; Exercise 10: Evaluating Housing Criteria can help you sort out your options to arrive at a decision.

Here are some of the alternatives you'll be considering:

- Present home
- Smaller single-family home
- Rental apartment
- Condominium or cooperative
- Duplex residence
- Retirement apartment
- Retirement community
- Campus plan or multifacility
- Retirement hotel or club
- Living with adult children or other relatives
- Mobile home

Residential Costs/Issues Checklist

These are the critical issues to consider when making the decision to relocate. Take special note of those which apply specifically to you.

- **Selling Price/Mortgage/Rent.** If a mortgage is necessary, the rate will be different from what you are used to paying since rates will have changed since you bought your present home. Rents can rise, particularly in very desirable areas; condominium dues and assessments can also rise quickly.

- **Cost of Living/Taxes.** Some retirees are lured from their homes to "low-cost, low-tax" areas; be aware that as an area becomes more popular, costs and taxes can rise to support the needs of a growing population. If selling your house, remember that you can postpone tax on any profit if you buy another principal residence within 2 years and you have lived in the house for 3 of the last 5 years. People 55 or older pay no tax on the first $125,000 of profit. This is a once in a lifetime tax-free provision.

- **Home/Car Insurance** may be less costly in a low-crime or less densely populated area, most costly in an urban or high-crime area.

- **Utility Rates** vary greatly from region to region and should be researched. Your bills can be reduced if you move to a small apartment, and can be reduced further if you're in an area with no dramatic seasonal changes. However, if you move to Florida from New York, for example, your air conditioning bills may offset decreased heating costs.

- **Repairs/Maintenance.** Do a thorough maintenance check of your home—what needs to be overhauled or replaced? Do you want to invest your time, money and energy on these problems or would you rather pass them on to someone else who welcomes the challenge?

- **Emotional Issues.** Are you prepared to move away from your home and all of its memories? Are you emotionally ripe for a change of environment, a new adventure?

- **Neighbors/Neighborhood.** Are you friendly with your neighbors? Have many of them become disinterested or moved away? Has the neighborhood maintained its attractive qualities, or has it become crowded, run-down, crime-ridden, or noisy? Is it a good neighborhood for retirees, or is it geared to young families or singles? How does your prospective new neighborhood rate in these areas?

- **Shopping/Services.** If you are considering a move to an isolated or sparsely populated area, the shopping areas may be considerably less extensive than those you are used to. Don't minimize the importance of convenience, particularly as you get older.

- **Health/Comfort.** Compare the number and location of doctors, hospitals and clinics in your present and prospective communities.

- **Transportation/Community Services.** You may now or in the future rely heavily on public transportation. Is it adequate where you live now or plan to live? Many retirement communities have their own buses for local transportation. Will visitors to your prospective home have easy access to an airport or bus terminal? Will you?

- **Climate.** Many retirees who move to warm climates find the summers unbearably hot. Consider the year-round climate and experience it, if possible, before moving. Many "snowbirds" go south in winter and north in summer, maintaining two residences or renting in one location.

- **Safety.** Will your present home be a safe one as you age? Are there potential hazards, such as steep stairs? What is the crime rate in your present/prospective community? Is the area very isolated? Do neighbors "look out" for each other?

- **Employment/Religious/Educational/Cultural Opportunities.** These may be limited if you move to a less populated community. How important are they to you? What does your present/proposed community have to offer?

Community Services

Community services become increasingly important in retirement. Find out about these services now, before a crisis hits: contact the following organizations (where you live now or where you plan to relocate) for information. After you fill in addresses and phone numbers, keep the listings as a reference.

- City (or area) Agency on Aging
  Address:
  Phone:

- Federal/State agencies (Social Security, Dept. of Labor)
  Address:
  Phone:

- Federal Information Center
  Address:
  Phone:

- Community Action Agency/Community Center
  Address:
  Phone:

- Public library
  Address:
  Phone:

- Local hotline
  Address:
  Phone:

- United Way or Community Chest
  Address:
  Phone:

- Public health offices
  Address:
  Phone:

- State/District Attorney's office
  Address:
  Phone:

- Local police/fire department
  Address:
  Phone:

- Professional associations
  Address:
  Phone:

- Senior centers
  Address:
  Phone:

- Community centers (YM/YWCA, YM/YWHA)
    Address:
    Phone:

- Religious organizations
    Address:
    Phone:

- A move to a more convenient type of housing in the same geographic area is often a good compromise solution: you are freed from the more onerous aspects of home maintenance and can stay in a familiar area.

- If you plan to improve your home or purchase major appliances, be aware that credit is often easier to obtain while you are (still) working.

- There are a number of federal, state and local programs that offer financial assistance to older homeowners; some states even reduce property taxes.

- Forty percent of women over the age of 65 are still living with their spouses; the percentage for men is higher because women have a longer life expectancy, on average. But, the prospect of living without one's spouse should be considered and planned for by both men and women. Figure 11, which follows, gives more complete data.

Networking for Relocation

You may remember from the chapter on working that one of the best ways to find a job is networking: contacting people you know who know others who can get you the information and connections you need. Similarly, networking is also one of the best ways to explore a new area to which you are considering relocating.

You may not know anyone who lives in Florida, but by talking to people you know, you can probably be referred to a mutual acquaintance who does, perhaps even in the very community you are considering. If you are considering a major move to a distant area, the ideal would be to phone your contact to arrange a personal visit during your trip to investigate the area. By planning an agenda for that meeting and preparing a list of questions, you can learn such things as:

- Types of housing available in the area
- Cost of housing, tax structure
- Community and health services available
- Climate at various points in the year, not just during your visit
- Accessibility to transportation, both public and long-distance (airports)
- Cultural and religious opportunities
- Desirability of area for retirees
- Disadvantages of living in the area for retirees
- Services or facilities which close down in the "off-season"

You will learn more from a networking contact than you can from any guidebook, since the contact has experienced year-round living firsthand in the region you're exploring. If the contact is unavailable to meet you in person, a well-structured phone interview is almost as good as a personal visit. However, at some point, you need to pay an extended visit to the area you are considering, at least a few weeks and ideally a month or more.

The fact that you enjoyed a vacation to the area for a week or two is not the same as living in that location long-term on a daily basis. And if you visited once during peak season, arrange for a visit at another time of year to get a flavor of the climate, pace of life and activities available at that time. The change can be quite dramatic!

Meeting Your (and Your Partner's) Needs

You must do your own planning and deciding on these housing issues. Your parents may have moved to Florida and love it, or George and Irma next door may have winterized their cabin in the woods and now spend all their time there, but that doesn't mean that these options are right for you.

The planning may be further complicated by your partner's needs. Just at the point your career may be winding down, your partner's may be revving up. This is fairly common with men who have worked 30 or 40 years and whose wives are younger and may have only worked full-time 5 or 10 years due to family responsibilities.

Each situation is unique, and only you can decide on the right course of action, either with your partner or by yourself if you don't have a partner. We have included a number of case studies to illustrate some typical examples. As you ponder each one, you will probably gain some insights into your own housing decisions.

Remember: Whether you stay put or make a major relocation, it's your move!

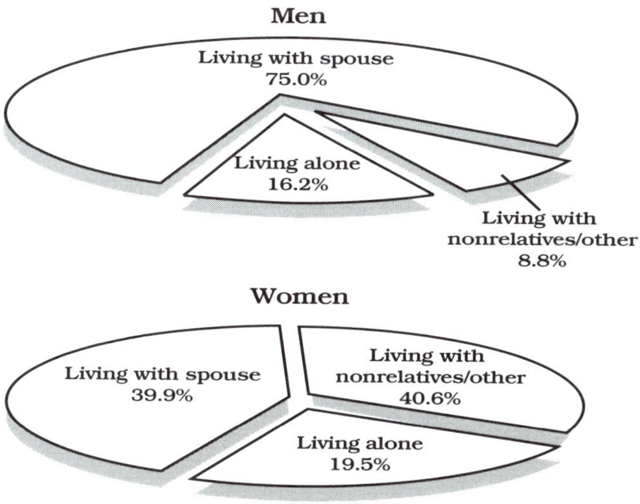

Figure 11 Living Arrangement for Individuals over 65
(Source: US Bureau of the Census, 1990)

Glossary of Housing Options for Older Americans

Accessory Apartment. A second, completely private living unit built within a single family home.

Boarding Home (Rooming House). Residential accommodation that usually consists of a bedroom/sitting room, private or shared bathroom, and common dining area. This housing is open to persons of all ages.

Condominium. Housing in an apartment building or townhouse complex in which individuals hold title to their living unit but share ownership of the common areas with other owners in the development.

Cooperatives. Non-profit corporations that own and operate a living facility for the benefit of the occupants who buy shares in the corporation in exchange for the right to occupy a specific living unit.

Congregate Housing (Sheltered or Enriched Housing). Specially planned, designed and managed multi-unit rental housing, typically with self-contained apartments. Supportive services such as meals, housekeeping, transportation, social and recreational activities are usually provided.

Conventional Home Ownership. Traditional ownership of a single family home, townhouse or manufactured (mobile) home.

Conventional Rental Housing. Traditional rental or leased housing in which tenants lease the right to occupy property—apartment or house—for a specific time at a specified cost.

Domiciliary Care Home (Personal Care, Residential Care). Group living arrangements that provide staff-supervised meals, housekeeping, personal care and private or shared sleeping rooms. These facilities are generally licensed and must meet design and operating standards, including minimum staff requirements.

Echo Housing (Elder Cottage, Granny Flat). A self-contained, free-standing, removable living unit occupied by a relative on the same property and adjacent to a single-family home.

Elderly Housing Project (Housing for Independent Elderly). Rental housing planned, designed and managed to meet the needs and interests of older tenants with services to support independent living.

Federally Assisted Housing (Public Housing). Rental housing built and operated with financial help from the Federal government and designed for low-income families of all ages. Some buildings have been specifically designed to meet the needs of low-income persons age 62 and over.

FHA/Veterans Administration/FHMA Home Loans. Federally insured home loan programs for the public and eligible veterans who want to purchase approved residential property.

Foster Care Homes. Single family homes in which non-related older persons live with a foster family. The family provides meals. housekeeping and personal care.

Homes for the Aged. Accommodations for the elderly with health limitations; they range from private homes that offer only custodial care to skilled nursing facilities. At a minimum, such homes provide private or shared sleeping rooms, meals, housekeeping and personal care and supervision.

Life Care Complex (Life Care Community, Continuing Care, Campus Complex). Housing development planned, designed and operated to provide a full range of accommodations and services for older adults, including independent living, congregate housing and medical care. Residents may move from one level to another as their needs change. Financial arrangements usually include a substantial entrance fee plus monthly charges.

Mobile Homes (Manufactured Housing). Compact, self-contained, factory-assembled housing units available for purchase or rental.

Rental Assistance (Housing Assistance, Section 8). Federal government program that provides financial assistance to older people and others with qualifying low incomes. No more than 25 to 30 percent of the individual's income goes toward rent in suitable housing.

Retirement Village (Retirement Community). Developments that typically offer home ownership and rental units for older people. Support services are often available for a fee.

Reverse Mortgage. One of the new financial plans designed to enable older homeowners to get cash for the equity in their homes while they continue to occupy them. Money is received in monthly payments or in lump-sum loans. The debt is outstanding for an agreed-upon number of years, sometimes until the house is sold.

Sale Leaseback. Another home equity conversion plan. A home is sold to an investor who immediately leases it back to the seller (older homeowner) for life.

Shared Home (Group Living). Arrangement in which three or more unrelated people share a house or an apartment. Usually private sleeping quarters are available; the rest of the house is shared.

*Source: *Housing Options for Older Americans*, AARP Publications, reprinted with permission of the publisher.

Case Study I: Tom and Margaret

Tom and Margaret have always enjoyed their annual 2-week winter vacation in North Carolina. They've gone to the same resort community for about 10 years, where they enjoy the ocean, restaurants and recreational activities.

They are considering selling their home in Massachusetts (where they have worked and lived for 25 years) and buying a house in a retirement community. Their son and his children live in the Northeast; their daughter and her children live in Florida.

1. What are some of the things Tom and Margaret should research and consider before committing to a permanent move to North Carolina?

2. What are Tom and Margaret's options besides an immediate, permanent move to North Carolina?

Case Study II: Carl

Carl is a widower living in a three-bedroom house. Since retiring, he's been spending much more time at home than he used to. He feels that the house is too big and that the maintenance and energy bills are too high; moreover, he no longer has the energy to do many of the repairs himself.

Carl's grown daughter, who lives 100 miles away, has suggested that Carl sell his house and move in with her family. He would have his own room, help with some expenses and repairs, and help with the care of her two school-aged children, with whom he has a good relationship.

Carl has been a member of the same church in his community for 18 years and has close friends with whom he plays golf regularly.

1. What issues should Carl discuss and consider regarding moving in with his daughter's family?

2. What other options does Carl have besides immediately moving in with his daughter's family?

Case Study III: Shirley

Shirley is 57 years old and lives alone in an apartment in a large city. Until her retirement a few months ago, she had worked steadily and was home only in the evenings and on weekends. Now, Shirley is home most of the time and realizes that her building is generally empty during the day. Many of the people Shirley used to see in the elevator, laundry room, or neighborhood grocery have moved; the new tenants are mostly young working couples.

Shirley still likes her neighborhood: it is near museums and concert halls, and she loves the arts. She has known the neighborhood butcher and dry cleaner ever since she moved in 17 years ago. However, her building superintendent is new and so is the corner grocer; she has not developed much of a relationship with either one. She does see some acquaintances in the park or while shopping, but because she worked such long hours, she never developed any deep friendships with her neighbors.

Shirley finds it disconcerting that even though the building is getting older and services are not as good as they used to be, rents have increased 30 percent in 4 years. And, while the neighborhood is pleasant by day and relatively safe, crime in the city has become a concern and she is apprehensive about walking alone at night.

Shirley's friend recently bought a small home in a semi-rural resort community that is several hours away from Shirley's apartment; her friend has suggested that Shirley buy a home in this community. Shirley has visited a few times and found it pleasant but isolated from the stimulation and culture of the city.

1. What are some of the things Shirley should consider as she contemplates this move?

____

____

____

2. What are Shirley's options besides staying in her current building and moving to her friend's community?

Case Study IV: Sam and Betty

Sam, 68, and his wife Betty, 61, retired from their jobs recently. Sam has experienced back problems and he has trouble walking. He does not look forward to the winter: the cold makes his back ache, and he is afraid of falling on slippery stairs and sidewalks.

Betty is in good health; upon retiring, she started a consulting business from her home. She has a large network of friends in her community, and several brothers and sisters with whom she has a close relationship live nearby.

The couple is considering a move to Florida, partly for Sam's health, but also because their only son and his family live there; Sam and Betty are only able to see them once a year. Wherever they live, Betty wants to continue to consult to businesses, and the couple wants to maintain contact with as many family and friends as possible.

1. What are some of the things Sam and Betty need to discuss and research in considering a move to Florida?

2. What other options are available to them besides a permanent move to Florida?

Exercise 10: Evaluating Housing Criteria

Review the various housing criteria; list those factors that are important to you; then, rank them using a scale of 1-5 (1=Most Important; 5=Least Important). When you are done, select the three most important criteria, and write brief sentences explaining how each will affect any final housing decision.

Finally, answer the questions on the next page.

Criteria	Rating
1.________________	______________________________
2.________________	______________________________
3.________________	______________________________
4.________________	______________________________
5.________________	______________________________

Most Important Considerations

1. ____

____

____

2. ____

____

____

3. ____

____

____

4. ____

____

____

5. ____

____

____

Questions

1. To what extent does your current housing meet your projected needs/desires? How can you modify your current housing to better meet these needs?

2. What other options might better meet your projected needs and desires?

3. What steps do you need to take to arrive at a final decision?

Lifetime Action Planning

9

What Will You Do?

Now that you've thoroughly analyzed every aspect of your retirement, it's time to do some action planning for the "third half" of your life. It's your life, and no one else can plan it or act on it for you. You can now set immediate goals based on what you've learned about yourself and your options. Briefly review each of these important considerations.

- **Finances.** Your plan should be made within the context of a well-considered financial plan. Housing, work and leisure decisions relate closely to your finances. Even if you've never used a financial planner or advisor, this may be the time to engage one.

- **Health.** You must assess your current state of health before you make any decisions. Be prepared to work toward maintaining your health, but you should also have a backup plan in case you have a health setback.

- **Time.** Your action plan will treat time as a resource, just like money or health. You will revisit the weekly time schedule you created earlier to modify it based on your greater knowledge of retirement planning. You will decide how much time you want to spend on each activity and schedule them accordingly.

- **Work.** In conjunction with your financial plan, you will decide if you want to work and how often. You will map out action steps to obtain work, if this is your choice. (We won't tell Maynard G. Krebs; he wouldn't have wanted to work at any age.)

- **Leisure.** You will plan meaningful, satisfying leisure activities that you can enjoy on your own and with others. They will not be limited to "traditional" retirement activities like golf, bingo and reading.

- **Roles, relationships, communication.** You will plan your activities so that you are spending the maximum amount of time in satisfying roles and relationships. You will use communication skills to define and manage your roles and relationships and to secure important retirement information.

- **Housing.** You will review your housing situation to decide if any action steps are necessary in this area to more effectively support your overall retirement goals.

Focus now on what you need to do to prepare for your first full year of retirement. It is strongly recommended that you review this plan at the end of the year, and create a new plan for the following year. The Activities Planning Chart is the first step in this process.

Writing the "Blue Print" for Your Future

You may find it easy to "fall into" some of your projected retirement activities, or you may be pursuing some of them already. However, there are activities that require planning, or "action steps." For instance, cross-country skiing may involve buying books on the subject, the selection and purchase of equipment, and research into the locations of good cross-country ski trails; for a Bachelor's Degree in Accounting, you'll need to look at course catalogs, research fees and prerequisite courses, pick a school offering quality instruction and a convenient schedule, and file an application by a certain date.

Steps in Your Action Plan provides a format that will help you set priorities and get your plans underway.

Developing Specific Goals

Earlier in the program, you developed a weekly schedule. Now that you've completed the program, look back at your planned activities: Is this a realistic schedule? Are all of your retirement goals represented? Are your priorities in order? Use the Weekly Time Chart done earlier as a basis for completing the Revised Weekly Time Chart.

Once you have revised your weekly schedule for your first year of retirement, you can build on that and plan for the longer future. Keep in mind that your interests and energy level will probably change in later years; this should be reflected in your future plans. For example, it may be unrealistic to plan a cross-country bicycle trek at age 75, but you might take shorter trips or develop your maintenance and repair skills.

Future Planning Ideas is a worksheet for planning activities beyond the first year.

Your New Beginning Starts Now

You've gathered a quantity of information on retirement issues and on your own goals, needs, interests and skills. You are ready to arrive at a complete life action plan for retirement. Use the Life Action Plan Narrative to write a brief description of your planned retirement for the first year. By forming a mental picture of your ideal retirement, you will have a target to aim at, and you will be more likely to hit that target.

The information and planning tools in this book should be useful throughout your retirement; we encourage you to refer to it frequently as a key resource. Earlier in this book, we compared retirement to the old gray mare. It certainly "ain't what it used to be." The possibilities and the challenge are endless. We've gone from rocking chairs and shuffleboard to marathons and mountain-climbing. Retirement was once a gradual ending; now it's a dramatic new beginning.

Drake Beam Morin is glad that we could help you arrive at your plan for this new beginning in your life. We wish you satisfaction and success in achieving it.

Exercise 11: Instructions for Activities Planning Chart

Look at the Activities Planning Chart which follows to start you thinking about your use of time. Add activities to those listed, or rearrange them according to your priorities.

Rate each activity with an A, B, or C to indicate level of interest.

A = Exciting
B = Moderately Interesting
C = Uninteresting

When you rate an activity "A," note what general interests, needs and skills might be satisfied by it.

If possible, compare your notes with your partner/spouse's choices, and look for any overlaps, contrasts and/or conflicts.

As a prelude to planning your first year of retirement, respond with a check mark to the questions "Doing It Now?" and "Want to Prepare?"

Rate each activity that interests you in terms of significant "Cost Factors."

L = Low Costs
M = Moderate Costs
H = High Costs

Check off the appropriate column if you can do the activity alone and/or with others (you may check off both columns for some activities). Which activities are congruent with your need to socialize or be by yourself? Review the amount of contact with people you currently experience in your job; how much will you expect and want during retirement?

In the "Planned Action" column, use a check mark to indicate if a substantial action plan is required. This will become part of your overall action plan. Start planning:

- *What to do to get started*
- *When you want to start*
- *How to allocate your time*

Activities Planning Chart

Activity	Interest level (A,B,C)	Self-assessment Interests/ Needs it meets	Doing it now?	Want to prepare?	Cost factors (L,M,H)	Doing it alone	With others	Planned action
1. Managing Finances Work on own								
Work w/financial planner								
Reading, study, seminars								
Lectures, correspondence courses								
On-campus courses								
Library research								
2. Health Golf, tennis, other sports								
Jogging, running								
Health club program								
Eliminate physical dependencies								
Improve diet								
Reduce stress								
3. Managing Time Take time mgm't course								
Prepare daily/weekly schedules								

Activities Planning Chart

Activity	Interest level (A,B,C)	Self-assessment Interests/ Needs it meets	Doing it now?	Want to prepare?	Cost factors (L,M,H)	Doing it alone	With others	Planned action
4. Work Running a business								
Consulting								
Part-time work								
Seasonal work								
Temporary work								
Full-time work								
5. Leisure Arts, crafts								
Collecting								
Carpentry								
Gardening								
Education/ Self-development								
Watch TV, listen to radio								
Movies, theater, dine out								
Read								
Museums, cultural pursuits								
Play cards, games								
Listen to music								

Activities Planning Chart

Activity	Interest level (A,B,C)	Self-assessment Interests/ Needs it meets	Doing it now?	Want to prepare?	Cost factors (L,M,H)	Doing it alone	With others	Planned action
5. Leasure (cont'd) Cruise or other travel								
Elderhostel/ Interhostel								
Volunteer work								
Other								
6. Roles, Relationships Communication Large gatherings								
Small groups								
Entertain at home								
Family gatherings								
Phone visiting								
Family talks								
Networking								
7. Housing Issues Yard work, projects								
Investigate relocation								
Housekeeping								
Bills/Taxes, desk work								

Action Plan

Look at the activities you have selected as possible alternatives for the first year; this exercise asks you to make tentative or actual commitments to begin them.

	Possible Activities	When I Want To Do It	What Action Steps I Will Take/ Start Date	Priority (A,B, or C)
1. Managing Finances	________ ________ ________	________ ________ ________	________ ________ ________	________ ________ ________
2. Health	________ ________ ________	________ ________ ________	________ ________ ________	________ ________ ________
3. Managing Time	________ ________ ________	________ ________ ________	________ ________ ________	________ ________ ________
4. Work	________ ________ ________	________ ________ ________	________ ________ ________	________ ________ ________
5. Leisure	________ ________ ________	________ ________ ________	________ ________ ________	________ ________ ________
6. Roles, Relation-ships	________ ________ ________	________ ________ ________	________ ________ ________	________ ________ ________
7. Housing Issues	________ ________ ________	________ ________ ________	________ ________ ________	________ ________ ________

Revised Weekly Time Chart

Complete the chart as you would like to spend a typical week in retirement. How creatively can you replace a 60-hour week of work-related activities? If participating with a spouse/partner, how much time will you now be spending together?

	Mon.	Tues.	Wed.	Thurs.	Fri.	Sat.	Sun.
8:00							
9:00							
10:00							
11:00							
12:00							
1:00							
2:00							
3:00							
4:00							
5:00							
6:00							
7:00							
8:00							
9:00							
10:00							
11:00							

Future Planning Ideas

Now that you have re-thought the use of time for the first year, what future planning ideas do you have? List activities that appeal to you for future years and project the date you most likely want to begin them.

	Possible Activities Beyond First Year	When I Am Likely to Begin	Action Steps to Take
1.			
2.			
3.			
4.			
5.			

Life Action Plan Narrative

Early in the program you were asked to briefly describe your retirement. Now it is time to pull together all your thoughts (with your spouse/partner, if appropriate) and write a brief description of your planned retirement for the first year.

1. *I/We* will be living in: (location, type of housing)

____

____

____

2. The most important new activities will be:

____

____

____

3. Principal travel plans for the first year will be:

____

____

____

4. The biggest capital outlay for the first year will be:

____

____

____

5. The biggest change anticipated in *my/our* relationship(s) will be:

____

____

____

6. Principal health and fitness activities will be:

____

____

7. Biggest concerns about this plan are:

____
____
____

8. *I/We* can begin to address these concerns by:

____
____
____

9. The parts of the plan *I am/we are* most comfortable with are:

____
____
____

10. During the first year, the major decisions *I/we* will need to make for the following year are:

____
____
____

Bibliography

American Association of Retired Persons. *Housing Options for Older Americans*. Washington, DC: AARP, 1984.

American Association of Retired Persons. *How to Plan for Your Successful Retirement*. Glenview, IL: Scott Foresman, 1988.

Ballard, Jack and Phoebe. *Beating the Age Game*. New York: Mastermedia, 1993.

Birsner, E. Patricia. *The Forty-Plus Job Hunting Guide*. New York: Simon and Schuster, 1987.

Bowman, Forest. *The Dollars and Sense of Estate Planning*. Englewood Cliffs, NJ: Prentice Hall, 1988.

Bridges, William. *Transitions*. New York: Addison-Wesley, 1980.

Chapman, Elwood. *Comfort Zones: A Practical Guide for Retirement Planning*. Los Altos, CA: Crisp Publications, 1985.

Charlesworth, Edward, and Ronald Nathan. *Stress Management*. New York: Ballantine Books, 1987.

Dychwald, Kenneth. *Age Wave*. New York: Bantam, 1990.

Ellison, James, et al. *Retiring on Your Own Terms*. New York: Crown, 1989.

Furman, Eleanor L. *Retirement: You're In Charge*. New York: Praeger, 1984.

Graedon, Joe and Teresa. *50 +, The Graedons' People's Pharmacy for Older Adults*. New York: Bantam Books, 1988.

Hardy, C. Colburn. *How to Retire Prosperously and Gracefully*. New York: J. K. Lasser, 1989.

Hendrickson, Mark L., and Gary Greene. *Exercise for Life: A Physical Activity Guide for the Athletic and Non-Athletic Retiree.* Phoenix, AZ: Health Plus Publishers, 1985.

Lakein, Alan C. *How to Get Control of Your Time and Your Life.* New York: McKay, 1990.

Lee, Alice and Fred. *A Field Guide to Retirement*. New York: Doubleday, 1991.

Levinson, Daniel L. *The Seasons of a Man's Life.* New York: Ballantine Books, 1976.

Mackenzie, R. Alec. *The Time Trap: How to Get More Done in Less Time.* New York: AMACOM, 1990.

Moran, Joan M. *Leisure Activities for the Mature Adult.* Minneapolis, MN: Burgess, 1979.

Myers, Albert, and Christopher P. Anderson. *Success Over Sixty.* Boston: G.K. Hall, 1985.

Nierenberg, Gerald, and Henry Calero. *How to Read a Person Like a Book.* New York: Pocket Books, 1989.

Procino, Jane. *Growing Older, Getting Better: A Handbook for Women in the Second Half of Life.* Reading, MA: Addison-Wesley, 1983.

Redd, Robert O. *Achievers Never Quit—How to Create a Life Plan for the Years After Fifty.* Ada, MI: Thornapple Press, 1989.

Salwen, Judy. *Solo Retirement: How to Make the Prime of Your Life the Time of Your Life.* New York: Dodd, Mead, 1983.

Shanaman, Fred. *The Best is Yet to Come: Retirement as a Career.* Seattle, WA: Outdoor Empire Publishing, 1984.

Shank, Howard. *Managing Retirement: The Surprising Opportunities and Challenges.* Chicago: Contemporary Books, 1985.

About Drake Beam Morin, Inc.

Drake Beam Morin, Inc. (DBM) is the world's leading organizational and individual transition consulting firm. DBM provides organizations and their employees with the highest caliber services and products available in the areas of employee selection, performance and transition management.

For almost three decades, we have assisted more than 70,000 organizations of all types and sizes and over five million individuals at all employee levels. This wealth of experience, which far surpasses any other firm in the industry, enables DBM to offer organizations the expertise that most effectively and efficiently meets their human resource challenges.

Through a network of over 150 offices around the globe, DBM provides personalized attention on a local level, along with a vast array of resources, wherever you may be located. With DBM, you have the best of two worlds: a local firm with global presence.

To find out more about how any of DBM's programs can benefit your organization, contact your local DBM office or DBM Corporate Headquarters, 100 Park Avenue, New York, NY 10017, 212 692-7700.

Notes

Notes